I am food

✝

I am food

✝

the mass in planetary perspective

Roger Corless

CROSSROAD • NEW YORK

1981
The Crossroad Publishing Company
575 Lexington Avenue,
New York, NY 10022

Printed in the United States of America

Library of Congress Cataloging in Publication Data

Corless, Roger.
I am food.

1. Mass.   I. Title.
BX2230.2.C67   264'.02036   81-7836
ISBN 0-8245-0077-6   AACR2

A SONG OF COMMUNION

I am Food I am Food I am Food;
I am the Eater I am the Eater I am the Eater;
I am the Eating I am the Eating I am the Eating;
I am Firstborn of the Worldforce;
I am prior to the gods;
I dwell at the Eye of the Deathless;
He who gives me is me indeed;
I am Food; the Foodeater I eat;
I have won the world and her spawning;
I am burning like the sun!
            Who knows this, knows Truth.

—*Taittirīya Upanisad* 3:10:5
(Translated by Roger Corless)

contents

WHY IS THE MASS? 11

Poem: "Christ on the Tree of Life" 20

**MASS, MYSTERY, AND THE IDOLATRY
OF RELEVANCE 21**

Verse: "Relevance" 27

THE PILGRIMAGE OF THE MASS 29

i am food

✝

why is the mass?

† in the name of god. amen.

Dylan Thomas wrote that, as a child, he was told everything about the wasp except why. Catholics learn a lot about the Mass, but they seldom learn why. The Mass, we are told, is a good thing. In the Middle Ages, some people thought it was such a good thing that they would go to two or three a day, and watch carefully for the elevation of the Bread. If one saw this often enough, it was believed, one would not only have a good harvest, but one would not become blind, so that one could keep on seeing the Bread. Conversely, not going was such a bad thing that one was assured of ending up in hell for a purposeful miss on Sundays and feasts.

Is there no more to it than that? Well, since you have picked up this book, and have discovered that it goes beyond the first paragraph, it should be clear that I at least think that there is a good deal more to it than that. For the Christian of any persuasion, the Mass (or Divine Liturgy, Holy Eucharist, or Lord's Supper) must be the center. Jesus did not say very much about prayer and meditation—most of the time he just lived it and expected us to catch on—but he did give us the Lord's Prayer and the Mass. The Lord's Prayer is intended as a model prayer, a kind of genetic template for all later Christian prayer (although, as we shall see, it presents great diffi-

11

culties of interpretation), and the Mass is a particularly poignant last will and testament, given on the night that a friend betrayed him to the police, which was somehow meant to be a summary of his life, his immanent death, and his coming resurrection and continued existence in the community of his followers and in the evolution and divinization of the earth.

Nobody could find such a thing boring. Yet many do. How can this be? Perhaps because we have never asked, "Why?." We go through the motions, but we do not watch what we are doing. Sometimes, we are not even sure of the motions. Someone at the front stands up. We all stand up. That someone decides he or she has made a mistake, and sits down. We all sit down, smirking at each other. Where are we? We should be at Mass, but we are daydreaming and waiting for it to be over, because we can't see much point in it.

I have been going to a Mass of one sort or another (as a Protestant, an Anglican, and now as a Catholic, and often as a visitor to Orthodox churches) for about thirty-five years now, and I have been asking myself "why" all the time. I asked myself, because when I asked the authorities—ministers, priests, parents—I received ambiguous and unsatisfactory answers all amounting to the assertion that it was a Good Thing. Yet there seemed to be a power in it, and no one was explaining that power to me. So I kept searching.

Now, I think, I have come up with an answer to the Why. It cannot be *the* answer, for the significance of any major spiritual activity must be constantly re-interpreted, and in the final analysis the only answer which makes sense is the answer which makes sense to *you*. I present here *my* answer, as I have it at the moment, and I think it is not a trivial answer, so it should help you to work out your own answer.

I became Catholic to my own surprise. I had been brought up a Protestant and I saw Catholics as strange creatures who went to a service which was called Mass because, it seemed clear to me, a mass of them were forced to go. As I matured, I found in Catholicism a curious *growing center* which had great power and potential, and I converted. That center brought together many insights which I had picked up from other religions, and moved them to a new synthesis. The synthesis was concentrated in the oddly named "Mass."

At first, I interpreted the Mass to myself along traditional lines. I had no other resources. Latin was still the language of the Mass, and the priest muttered it with his back toward us. I read everything I could on it, including *The Mass of the Roman Rite Described* by Fortescue and O'Connell. It gave as much detail on the ritual as the automobile maintenance manual gives for my car.

Had I read no further, this book would be another in the series of excellent, but ultimately claustrophobic, devotional books on "the spiritual meaning of the Mass." Fortunately, I discovered Buddhism. If you ever thought you understood anything, try Buddhism. It questions even the very organ of investigation, the mind, which it calls Ignorance. As Firesign Theater puts it, "Everything you know is Wrong." Buddhism destroys our intellectually constructed walls and foundations, and leaves us floating in Emptiness.

After plunging into Emptiness, nothing can ever be dogmatically certain again, but neither can anything ever be purely relative, for Relativism is itself a dogma. A strange freedom appears. Freedom from, and freedom for. Freedom from tradition, and freedom for tradition.

Three books on the Mass I have found helpful: a chatty little thing by Monsignor Ronald Knox, *The Mass in Slow Motion*; an essay of strangely aseptic passion called "The Mass on the World" by Father Pierre Teilhard de Chardin; and a treasure trove of detailed but often unintelligible insights by the Orthodox scholar Nicholas Cabasilas, *A Commentary on the Divine Liturgy*. I am somewhat influenced by all three, yet I depart from all of them. Knox's book is a collection of sermons which he gave to English Catholic schoolgirls during World War II (it was published in the United States by Sheed and Ward, New York, 1948). The species of human which made up his congregation was a giggly, ink-stained, and freckly variety which used the word "jolly" a lot and has nothing very much in common with the modern American or English Catholic. However, Knox's attempt to describe the inner meaning of "his" Mass, rather than lecturing on liturgics, was a jolly good idea, and I have adopted it.

Pierre Teilhard de Chardin had the misfortune of thinking a little ahead of the Vatican. Like a submissive wife in some cultures, we are supposed to follow a few steps behind, even if we feel that our husband has lost his way. Nowadays, of course, de Chardin is much in favor, since he took the precaution of dying before having his banned works published. He saw the Mass in a cosmic setting. It happened that he was in the middle of Nowhere at a time when he did not have the materials to say Mass. Actually, he was in the middle of China, which the Chinese have always considered to be the center of civilization, but Father de Chardin was a Frenchman of impeccable taste, and he quite properly regarded himself as surrounded by barbarians. How could he fulfill his priestly obligation to say daily Mass? Fortunately for us, he was not like me, and he did not give up on the idea and do Buddhist meditation instead, as I did when "stranded" one Sunday at Bodh Gaya, the place of the Buddha's Enlightenment, with not a church in sight. He resolutely said Mass, but did so by visualizing *the world as a sacrament*. The resulting document (see *Hymn of the Universe*, New York: Harper, 1965, pp. 19-37) is full of powerful images ("In the beginning there was the *Fire*") and strange requests ("Lord, let no wine befuddle me"). He bequeathed us a stirring image of the Mass as a cosmic event, which I would like to work through in my own way, but he was rather quick to dismiss "the pagans," from whom I have learned much.

Nicholas Cabasilas, who lived obscurely around the fourteenth century somewhere in the Byzantine Empire, pro-

duced studied reflections upon the Mass, which the Orthodox churches call the Divine Liturgy, trying to penetrate the
mystical significance of each and every act of the priest and
people (*A Commentary on the Divine Liturgy*, translated by
J.M. Hussey and P.A. McNulty; London: S.P.C.K., 1978).
His remarks are often profound, but they seem to assume
that the Orthodox liturgy is of itself divine and therefore
unalterable. They show no appreciation for historical development, and today they have a musty, if fascinating, quality
like a trunk of memorabilia discovered in an attic.

None of these books, despite their obvious spirituality,
takes very much notice of "the pagans." One is left wondering if God created them by mistake. What about all those
people "out there"? John Henry Cardinal Newman suggests
an answer. A hapless man known to history only as "Mr.
Millman" made the mistake of criticizing Newman's choice of
Roman Catholicism over the Church of England, which the
pitiable Millman identified as Protestantism. Protestants,
claimed Millman, were the true Christians because they had
the "pure Gospel" unmixed with "pagan accretions" such as
images, incense, celibate priests, and sacrifices. The wretch-
ed Millman discovered that he had called the fighting Cardinal out of his corner wielding Millman's own weapons.
"Mr. Millman," snorted Newman, "claims that these things
are in paganism, therefore they are not Christian. On the
contrary, we claim that these things are in Christianity,
therefore they are not pagan."

There is a very important principle at stake here. Some
Christians have argued that true Christianity can be recognized by its *differences* from other religions. The distinguished
Protestant theologian Karl Barth, who has produced an
enormous work intimidatingly called *Church Dogmatics*
argues strenuously for this position. He even wishes to keep
the word "religion" for non-Christian religions, which are, to
him, human constructions, and differ radically from True
Evangelical, or Barthian, Christianity, in every respect. Chris-

tianity comes directly from God, more or less complete in all
its parts, like a TV dinner.

But something is fishy about the logic here. If the True Religion is different *in every respect* from all other religions, then
it would be unrecognizable as a religion at all. It would be like
an alien life-form on some distant planet which we might discover without recognizing that it was a life-form. In the much
underrated Russian movie *Solaris*, the alien life-form is a
lake, and it is quite some time before the humans realize that
the lake is trying to communicate with them. Now, how is it
that everybody except Barth happily recognizes Christianity,
even the severe Barthian kind, as religious? And then again,
the logic requires that, were I to make a list of the contents of
all known religions, and then make a further list of everything
that was not in the first list, I would come up with a Christianity that was truer than the Truth according to Barth. As a matter of fact it would be fairly easy to argue, on this basis, that
Mahāyāna Buddhism is the True Evangelical Christianity,
since Mahāyāna Buddhism is so adept at escaping from la-
bels it cannot readily be called anything at all.

The most serious difficulty with the Barthian position is a
practical one. If God is the Great Provider, who sends me TV
dinners when I am hungry, and does not let me forage and
cook for myself, it means that neither God nor myself is very
much at home here. We have found Planet X, and it is this
one. And the sooner we get off it and go to heaven, the better. It does not much matter if we destroy this alien planet
with its funny little nonhuman life-forms. How on earth the
Incarnation, the wrapping of God in our substance so completely that he became one of us, fits into such a picture quite
escapes me.

The Catholic God is a much happier God than this one.
He likes his creation, he cares as much for the flu virus as for
Karl Barth. He laughs a lot. We have not always remembered
this, and the artists in the Middle Ages made him look especially grim. This was because they paid too much attention to

God's transcendence—and this may also be Barth's problem. The Christian God is transcendent, immanent, personal, and transpersonal, all at the same time. In a real sense, the
history of theology is the history of trying to make this incomprehensible Trans-Entity fit into a neat, comprehensible
world-view. The attempt is doomed to failure from the beginning, but that does not mean that we should give up. If we
say nothing, nothing will be said (as Calvin Coolidge might
have put it). So we must say something, but take our cue
from Buddhism and realize that any statement about ulti-
mates is partial and can be no more than *helpfully false.*

The mention of Buddhism brings us back to Newman. The
unfortunate Mr. Millman had overemphasized God's transcendence. Newman argued for his immanence. The Qur'ān
says, "Allah is nearer to you than your jugular vein" and St.
Augustine wrote that God is closer to us than we are to ourselves. The sort of God who would become incarnate is one
who is so bound up with his creation that he is *already inside
it.* This mode of God is technically called the *Logos*, a Greek
word meaning "ordered expression" (hence the English
word "logic") which we rather weakly translate as "The
Word." Wherever there is ordered expression, there is God.
The Greek word for order is *cosmos*, and it is the opposite of
chaos, out of which *cosmos* came. Ever since creation, of
course, there has been *cosmos*. So, ever since creation,
there has been God inside everything *as well as* (and this dis-
tinguishes monotheism from monism) outside everything.
We cannot drop out of God. This God is everywhere wor-
shipped, even by so-called atheists, so long as a person lives
without hypocrisy according to the truth as he or she sees it.
And this is the God who became the man Jesus.

If this idea is new to you, go back and read John 1:1-18
and realize that this is what the evangelist wants to say. Augustine remarked that he had learned the doctrine of verses 1
through 13 from his paganism. Verse 14, "the Word became
flesh," was the bombshell that converted him. Now, he dis-

covered, he did not have to peer into the nature of things or
to go up to the seventh heaven to see God. God had walked
our planet and left a record of his sayings and doings. And it
is *this* Christ, the enfleshment of the *universal ordering principle*, who said "no one comes to the Father except through
me" (John 14:6). That is to say, from this point of view, *all
religions and ideologies are implicitly Christian*. Some are
quite close to Christianity (such as Judaism) and some are so
distant from it (such as Nazism) that we find the face of Christ
there only in a shattered and horribly distorted form.

We might think of God as the curator of a museum called
the Church. From the beginning of creation, through the
history of Israel and of the Church, God has been collecting
choice pieces and putting them in his museum. The Church,
however, is not a museum (though I sometimes think the
Vatican would prefer it to be!); it is an *organism* called the
Body of Christ. So we can change the image and think of
God eating the pieces he collects, taking them into himself,
literally *incorporating* them. So, for instance, many non-
Christians worship in front of images. The Jews were not allowed to, because God had revealed himself as beyond images (according to the developed tradition which became
standard). But Christ was a man and, although we have no
early pictures of him, he must have looked, at the least, like a
male human being. It is then permissible for Christians to
worship before an image of Christ. Neither Christians nor
non-Christians (a point which the Old Testament gets
thumpingly wrong) are worshipping the images themselves.
Anybody of average intelligence, no matter what his or her
culture is, has no trouble realizing that a statue as a statue
cannot move around or speak or eat. The statue is like a picture of a friend: it is a door to his or her personality, through
which the personality is actually felt to pass, and one may
honor the picture as if it were the friend. A wife, for example,
may kiss the photograph of her absent husband, and we all
know that she knows that we know that the photograph is not
her husband.

One could go down the list of non-Christian things and show how they have been Christ-ed into the Church. The main point, however, is how this action takes place. When God became man as Christ, say many of the Church Fathers, he not only took on our flesh, he took on all humanity, indeed he took on everything earthly. This is easier to see today, when we have discovered how we are so much like the rest of the planet. Pulled apart and labeled, we come out as about 90 percent water and a few dollars' worth of rather ordinary chemicals. Christ, then, took on the vesture of the seas, the mountains, the fish, and the birds, as a necessary consequence of taking on what Buddhists remind us is "a skin bag of bones oozing excrement from its nine openings." The world itself is now divinized because it formed the robe of the Godman.

The burning focus of this divinization is Christ himself, now pictured as "sitting on the right hand of the Father," that is, Christ as Victor over sin and death, pulsating at the center of the Unapproachable Light. This fire has been committed into the keeping of the Church, which dispenses it through the sacraments, particularly the Mass. This is "why" the Mass is. It is our window on eternity, the cool fire of the living Christ who draws us all up, if we let him, into his own divinity. Becoming divine ourselves (by adoption, not by right, it is most important to note), we then participate in the divinization of our planet, acting as the cosmic priests which was our destiny from the beginning, blessing the animate and the inanimate, assisting everything to grow into the unimaginable full stature of Christ.

In order to help you to see something of this, of the cosmic centrality of the Mass, I will combine the approaches of Knox, de Chardin, and Cabasilas, with my own deep interest in other religions, especially Buddhism, to give you an account of "my" Mass which might make sense of "your" Mass. From Buddhism, I will take the idea of entry into the mandala, with its attendant notions of a progress in our relationship to God from the position of a servant, through the status of a friend, to the final divinization itself.

But first, I want to say something about why so many
Masses today are boring.

CHRIST ON THE TREE OF LIFE

The Host this morning
tastes of Spring moss,
dew, lichens and fertile dankness:
and here it is no longer
church, altar, priest and people,
but forest,
stones, sun and squirrels
straining together
for joy at the nonstop
uprush of life
prodigally spawning
death, change and process.

Who loves God well enough
to take up serpents
and not be harmed,
to stand in the rain
and grow by it?
For whom
is the earth with her creatures not strange,
only the clothed apes odd,
who strain competitively
to fly with angels
and fall
to a subanimal isolation?

Evolution,
in part random,
in total planned,
moves inscrutably as snakes
to its unspoken consummation,
the Word yet unpronounced.

mass, mystery, and the idolatry of relevance

Recently I took a practical course in Tibetan Buddhism. One of the things we had to do was to gather early in the morning and chant a liturgy for an hour in Tibetan. Few of us knew the language, so we were given a phonetic transcription, but not, at first, an English translation. The lama said that making the sounds was quite sufficient to change our consciousnesses. I watched with some fascination as a roomful of intelligent people devoutly made, day after day, what were to them unintelligible noises. They did not think it at all odd.

I am old enough to remember when Mass was something like that. At a simple Mass, which we used to call Low Mass, the priest would mumble in Latin, only occasionally raising his voice to an audible level, turning toward us to see if we were still there, or saying something in English. The congregation took to this procedure quite happily and, at the end of the largely silent ceremony, was confident that it had "heard Mass."

Then someone decided that this was not Relevant. People were drifting away from the Church, it was said, because its liturgy had become mere formalism. Were we to tighten up the show, explain everything, and put it all in English, the lapsed would return in droves. But they didn't. They went off to do Zen, Yoga, and Tantra, and earnestly chanted in Japanese, Sanskrit, and Tibetan. The Church decided to downplay incense, rosaries, and elaborate vestments, so as to become Relevant. Young Catholics went off to Buddhism and Hinduism, where incense, rosaries, and elaborate vestments are the order of the day. Older Catholics, who did not wish to leave the Church, found a champion in Archbishop Lefebvre, for whom Relevance is irrelevant.

I once saw a bookmark designed by some earnest person which said simply RELEVANCE! Where did this idol come from? I believe it has no one source, but its appearance is a symptom of a deep sickness in our modern society. As a Greek Orthodox woman said to me, after I had attended Divine Liturgy and she had discovered I was Catholic, "Ah, yes, the Catholics. They have lost the mystery." Or as Jung said, we concentrate too much on reason and the waking consciousness, and we ignore dreams and the subconscious, in which we spend at least a third of our lives.

A crisis I see in today's Catholicism is the sharp split between traditionalists and liberals. Traditionalists want to keep everything, liberals want to change everything. Traditionalists retreat to the pre-Vatican II Latin Mass (the mumbled one), while Liberals organize an Assumption procession dressed as tomato soup cans and carrying (I swear I saw this reported) a sign saying "Mary is the greatest tomato of them all." Both camps seem to me to be hooked on preconceived ideas. Buddhism shows us that preconceived ideas lead to fanaticism and then to suffering when our precious ideas are opposed or defeated. As a Zen Master once said to me, "In Zen, must have soft head. Not have hard head." That is, our ideas must flow so as to be appropriate to the situation.

I think the difficulty began in the Europe of the late Middle Ages. At that time, scholars started to do taxonomy, to classify things, in a serious way. The idea was to discover how the God of order had arranged the universe, to understand what it was with which we had to deal in our everyday lives. This laudable enterprise had two curious, and quite opposite, effects which could not have been foreseen at the time.

On the one hand, science began to be put on a sure footing. Previously, everyone had followed Aristotle, whom they called simply The Philosopher, who had written a lot about science but had never done any experiments worth noting. That might not have mattered, since Einstein never did any experiments worth noting either, except that *nobody else* did any experiments to test his theories. For instance, he said that heavier bodies fall faster than lighter ones. That seems reasonable enough if you just think about it, but in fact it turns out that if you try it you find that everything falls at the same rate, so long as it happens in a vacuum where gravity is the only significant factor. Galileo got into trouble not because he thought, but because he looked. He refused to accept armchair dogma, and went for observation as the only admissible way to obtain data.

Taxonomy led to the birth of science as a distinct endeavor of the human mind. In it, practice was the basis of theory. But taxonomy also led, on the other hand, to the increasingly minute classification of religion into different activities. An activity called Mystical Contemplation was identified and labeled as distinct from ordinary, everyday ethical practice and Massgoing. Mystical Contemplation became more and more special until it eventually was put on a high shelf reserved for the "great mystics," which usually meant dead ones. Ordinary, living mortals like you and me who claimed any mystical insights were treated like naughty children who had stood on a chair to reach the cookie jar. Yet even a cursory reading of the New Testament shows that the early Christians were high on Christ much of the time. When martyrdom was in fashion, Christians would be so intoxicated with the presence of God that they would rush into the lions' arena, and many pagan soldiers who saw this were so impressed that they would rush in too, later to be put on the roll of saints among those who had received the "baptism of blood."

Early Christianity was based upon observation. Some people claimed that they experienced Christ as God. When other people prayed to Christ as God, on a sort of bet (there were many candidates for God at the time), they found that they also experienced Christ as God, or at any rate as somebody superhuman. From these experiences, refined and tabulated by the community of experiencers (the Church) in a rational and scientific way, Christian doctrine emerged, and false conclusions (heresy) were distinguished from true ones (orthodoxy). The laboratory of these experiences was prayer, or, which is or should be the same thing in Christianity, meditation. When meditation came to be labeled as an activity separate from ordinary Christianity, the doctrines of ordinary Christianity began to seem arbitrary, so that today we are presented with lists of doctrines and practices unsupported by experience. One of these lists, called the Nicene Creed, we recite at Mass. I shall look at that in some detail later.

For now, let us just notice what a strange thing happened in or about the eleventh century. Science, which had been all theory and no practice, that is, all dogma, united theory and practice, and so became credible. Religion, which had been a union of theory and practice, split and produced a set of unreasonable dogmas and arbitrary practices. People are therefore more impressed by science and Eastern religions, in both of which theory and practice are kept in balance, than they are by Christianity.

The modern obsession with Relevance sees this split, but does not, I think, see it aright. It wants to make Christianity Relevant by explaining everything. But this will not work. As St. Thomas Aquinas said, God cannot be *comprehended* by reason, but he can be *apprehended* by love.

The distinction between comprehension and apprehension implies a more noble model of consciousness than the one we customarily use. In many religions, indeed perhaps all religions, consciousness is a two-level affair. Ordinary consciousness uses reason, and gets us through the day. But superconsciousness transcends reason, without denying or annihilating it, and knows the unicity of God directly. This, I think, is what Aquinas calls "love." It is a "feeling-knowing" (I am told that there is an Indonesian word that means "to see with the eye of feeling") which is not a blind faith nor is it in

any way imprecise, but it is not amenable to compartmentali-
zation and labeling. It knows the Mystery, a word which
comes from a Greek root meaning "with the closed lips," i.e.,
verbally inexpressible.

We have today lost touch with this upper storey of our consciousness. Any deviation from the normal ability to get
through the day is automatically labeled madness, without
regard to its destructive or constructive elements. Freud considered mysticism to be mild schizophrenia. If we restore con-
fidence in our upper storey (Jung would perhaps call it a
lower storey, but both words signify an ignored portion of our
consciousness), we can solve the question of Relevance.

What we have lost is not Relevance but Mystery. When the
priest shows up for Mass and announces brightly, "Hi! I'm Father O'Shea? Let us all confess our sins according to Form
B," we do not feel the lack of Relevance; indeed we feel in-
vaded by Relevance, but we do feel the absence of Mystery.
Everything is too ordinary. How does the Mass differ from a
coffee hour?

The idolatry of Relevance leads to banality, because it de-
grades superconsciousness to mere consciousness. Superconsciousness works on consciousness via symbol, suggestion, art, ritual, since it seeks self-transcendence and needs
an equivocal, evocative, transformative language. Consciousness is an affair of "1" and "0," a strict, univocal, computer language which informs but does not transform. Both
levels are valuable, but they have different uses. Consciousness helps us to fill out our tax returns. Superconsciousness
helps us to contact God.

Confusion results from the muddling of these levels, either
by reducing God-language to computer language, or by answering with a poem a question about one's income tax. If I
say that God is one, I mean it in terms of superconsciousness.
In terms of consciousness, it would mean that God was either
1 or 0. But this is nonsense. I may count up all the cockroach-
es in the room, and find that there is 1 or 0, but it cannot

mean anything to count up gods and find that there is 1. As
the Upanishads say, God is One without a Second, that is, he
is a nonmathematical One who is not part of a series 1, 2, 3,
etc. As soon as we begin to count, says St. Augustine, we
have lost the Trinity.

Every good symbol has two heads. One looks at us, at our
world, and the other looks at the beyond. A symbol is a vehicle for transcending our ordinary consciousness. A symbol
which does not do this is only a sign. The golden arches of
McDonald's signify hamburgers, but it is only in the fantasy
world of the TV commercial that they transport us into ecsta-
sies. They are a Pavlovian stimulus to salivate (or not to, de-
pending on our predisposition to McDonald's hamburgers).

When a symbol is degraded to a sign, it loses the head that
looks beyond, and it gazes inanely at us alone. This, I feel, is
the source of the present banality in so many of our Masses. I
could tell many horror stories of this degradation. Here are
just a few. Most of them occured in California, where the
motto seems to be Relevance or Bust.

It was the First Sunday of Advent. We had all dutifully arrived for Mass, but the Church was locked. After we had
milled about for a time and begun to wonder if we should eat
breakfast instead, the priest unlocked the church and let us
in. When we were seated, he explained that "Advent is a
time of waiting." Therefore, when I went on Ash Wednesday
and found the walls covered with aluminum foil, I realized at
once that Lent is a time for reflection. On Maundy Thursday,
I went to a Mass at a Protestant church that had been requisi-
tioned for the night by some very with-it Catholic seminarians
and their trendy teachers. A gentleman in leotards, whom I
hoped was a priest, sat cross-legged in the center of the
church and sang cheery little songs as he picked up and re-
placed a glass of wine and a plate of bread. At one point I
turned to the person next to me who, despite her elaborate
disguise as a laywoman, was obviously a nun, and voiced my
suspicion. "Sister, did we just have the Consecration?"

"Ooh, yes," she affirmed, "and isn't it just *wonderful?*" And then there is the weekly spectacle of the priest inviting us to "join with the song of the angels in heaven," at which the folk with guitars strike up and, bobbing up and down like the introduction to the Muppet Show, sing "Holy, Holy, Holy . . . ," whereupon I devoutly hope that the music of the angels is more sublime, or I will convert to Sikhism, wherein they say that God can be approached only by music, never by concepts.

RELEVANCE

A hearty Modern Liturgist,
all his cheeks a-tremble,
loudly shakes me by the hand:
"Jesus is our Chum!"

All of this, I think, is a reaction against the grimly transcendent picture of God in the Middle Ages. We are trying to rediscover his immanence, which is good, but in the process we are losing his transcendence, which is bad, and those who feel the loss of transcendence overcompensate in the other direction by using the Tridentine Mass or chanting in Tibetan. In his transcendence, God dwells in unapproachable light, and is infinitely distant. This aspect is expressed in mumbled Masses and inexplicable paraphernalia. But in his immanence, God is nearer to us than we are to ourselves, and this aspect is expressed in the intimacy of our personal communions. When either aspect is overemphasized, we are no longer in contact with the fullness of the Christian God, and we feel a spiritual lack.

The Tridentine Mass, beloved of Archbishop Lefebvre, emphasizes the transcendence, and the Vatican II Mass, which the rest of us use, emphasizes the immanence. Either Mass can give us the feeling of authenticity only if it proceeds from a center of genuine spirituality. Our priests are presently taught how to operate a church, but they are seldom taught

how to meditate. As a result, they do an effective job, but
many of them seem shallow. This was not so obvious when
they mumbled the Mass in Latin, for the very mumbling was
somehow magical. But if you got up close, as I did occasionally, what you heard was not Latin at all but a sequence
of Latinesque syllables strung together as quickly as possible.
Now that the Mass is in English, we see the reality. Far too
many priests are Mass-sayers, and far too few know why they
are saying Mass.

Every now and then, of course, we find a Mass which inspires us. But mostly we do not. In this situation, when the
priests have by and large lost the Mystery, it is up to us laypeople to retrieve it. The priest is the chairman of the Mass
but not the dictator. We are also priests (I Peter 2:5,9). It is
necessary for us to question the whole system that subjugates
one Christian to another in a bureaucracy developed in the
Middle Ages. At that time, perhaps it made sense. The power
pyramid was the only model of authority that they had. But
today we must ask what it means that one of the Pope's titles,
the one historically least emphasized, is "Servant of the Servants of God." Does it mean a democracy of the indwelling
of the Holy Spirit, whose actions are from time to time as-
sessed by external witnesses? It is not my intention here to
argue for a radically new church order, but to suggest that we
cannot supinely await directives from above which will
change our lives: we must take action ourselves. We must
discover God in ourselves and in our fellow creatures, and
we must bring this discovery to our own Mass. That way, it
can never be boring. And it will be truly "relevant."

the pilgrimage of the mass

If *It's Tuesday, This Must Be Belgium* was the title of a movie some years ago about a group of Americans on a sitcom group tour through Europe. The title nicely points out the difference between a *journey* and a *pilgrimage.*

A pilgrimage is a religious journey. But that does not get to the heart of the matter. What does "religious" mean in this context? It implies a sense of order and ultimate purpose which transcends secular concerns. A journey is an attempt to get from spot A to spot B, both of which are locatable in ordinary space, in the shortest amount of ordinary time possible, so as to perform some limited objective such as visiting a friend, concluding a business deal, or taking a trip.

A pilgrimage is also an attempt to go from spot A to spot B, both of which are locatable in ordinary space, but there the resemblance with a journey stops. A pilgrimage is not concerned to take the shortest time between the two points. It may even seek for the longest time. Sometimes, pilgrims crawl toward their goal on hands and knees. Recently, two Americans who had become monks of a Chinese Buddhist monastery in San Francisco, completed a pilgrimage down the West coast in the traditional Chinese manner: one monk walked in normal fashion, carrying the life-support provisions, while the other proceeded according to the difficult method of "three steps, one bow"—three steps, a double genuflection all the way to the ground, then three more steps, and so on.

Clearly, on a pilgrimage, it is not only better to travel than to arrive, but if one does not travel properly, one does not really arrive. This is because the goal is not merely a geographical location, it is also a sacred center. It is the center of

29

the pilgrim's world. For a baseball fan, the center might be the Baseball Hall of Fame, or the stadium of her favorite team. The person's life revolves around that space. For a Muslim, it is Mecca, to which he is bound to go, if possible, at least once in his life. The word *Mecca* has entered our language, since Muslims are the world experts at pilgrimage, so that we sometimes say "the Hall of Fame is the baseball fan's Mecca." Many religions and ideologies have their Mecca.

A journey to the center of the earth is a serious matter. One expects to meet there not only the core of the world but also the core of one's own being. *A pilgrimage is a journey to the center of Meaning.* A Muslim's world does not make sense without Mecca. When he reaches it, he is integrated with his world and with himself. Such a journey cannot be undertaken lightly. It must be done slowly, recollectedly, savoring the sense of occasion. And its movement is both outward and inward at the same time. This movement is technically called "enantidromia," mirror-image-movement. If we want to enter a mirror, we step away from it and our image goes in more deeply. This, it seems to me, is a law of the spiritual life. In order to do we must non-do, as the *Tao Te Ching* repeatedly says. He who loses his life gains it. To find the God within, the Logos slumbering in our souls, we have to go to a place "out there."

Where is the Christian's sacred goal? In a sense, it is Israel (the "Holy Land") and Jerusalem, for that was the earthly stage for the life of Jesus. But Christians are not bound to this territory in the sense that Jews are. We are citizens of "the Jerusalem above;" we have here no abiding city, no necessary geographical center (Hebrews 13:14). Our center is Christ, who had nowhere to lay his head (Matthew 8:20), yet now "fills all in all" (Ephesians 1:23).

The center of pilgrimage is sometimes called a mountain. This is so even in Islam, where the "mountain" is a slight depression. The sacred center *feels like* a mountain and *feels like* the center of the earth, in the feeling-thinking of superconsciousness. It is not necessary that it be geographically and physically a mountain at the center of the earth. The central sacred mountain is, for Christians, the Mass, wherever it happens to be said. Our progress through the Mass is a pilgrimage toward and up the placeless Mountain on whose summit is Christ. It is a journey outward (to a church building and to its altar) and a journey inward (to personal communion with Christ). It is a progress to the center of meaning, not a meaningless moving around ("If It's Tuesday, This Must Be Belgium").

I want to speak of this pilgrimage, of how it comes alive for me, in five parts of unequal length: setting out, entering the mandala, speech, food, and living in the mandala. We begin the pilgrimage as servants, we grovel a little. After we have entered the mandala, we approach God as friends. At Communion we enter into God as he enters into us and experience a transpersonal trans-emotion which Tantric Buddhists call Pride of Deity. We leave, trying to preserve this state as long as possible, seeing the Mandala of Christ everywhere.

A. SETTING OUT

There is a distressing Catholic habit of "catching" a Mass. "I'll catch the eight o'clock so I can be on the golf course by nine." This cheapens the Mass to a kind of magic pill. It is a pill on which we are hooked, for we do not feel better when we have taken it, but we feel very bad if we do not take it. Childhood visions of the mouths of hell closing upon the delinquent, thundered out at us by Sister Tarantula, simmer beneath our adult calm.

We should no more feel that we "have" to go to Mass than we should feel that we "have" to accept a good friend's invitation to dinner. Mass is supposed to be a joyful occasion, and we should want to go just to get in on the cosmic action. There may be Sundays when it is just not possible to go, and then we should feel a sense not of guilt but of loss. Eastern

Orthodox Churches take this view: the earnest Christian will show up at liturgy because it is rather grand, and there is no need to dragoon people into reluctant attendance. Perhaps Catholics have the Sunday Mass rule because Mass is so seldom grand.

The story is told of the Czar when he had decided to make Russia a Christian country. He sent envoys to report on the two contending varieties of Christianity, at Rome and at Constantinople. The envoys went first to Rome and attended papal High Mass. They were dazzled, and decided that Catholicism would be the religion of Russia. For the sake of the Czar's orders, however, they went on to Constantinople (called Istanbul today) for the Divine Liturgy celebrated by the Patriarch. This so overwhelmed them that they remarked later "We knew not whether we were in heaven or on earth," and so Russia became Orthodox.

I find a steady diet of Orthodox liturgies somewhat rich for my taste, and I am glad of the simpler options provided by Catholicism. But, being human, we tend to get lazy and take the simpler option all the time. There is much truth in Gibbon's malicious remark that "the Church of Rome is naught but the ghost of the Roman Empire, crowned and sitting upon the grave thereof." The Roman Empire excelled in law and administration, and all I can remember from high school days about its history is a picture of a roomful of bald clones wearing sheets and plotting how to get more land and rule it into dullness.

Law is antithetical to creativity and spirituality. It does not give us a vision of what might be; it tells us the bare minimum that we *must* do in order to stay out of jail (or hell). Since Catholicism has paid so much attention to law, it has been very ingenious in telling us how little we need to do, and in suppressing our creativity.

The situation after Vatican II is worse than before it. Previously, there was, for instance, a rule to observe every Friday as a mini-Lent. This was to be done by abstaining from meat, so, to the delight of the fishmongers, Friday was fish day. But since the rule was just a rule, many people observed it without any real devotion, and became very upset if they thought they saw a piece of meat in their vegetable soup. Then they had to consult their confessor, for canon law had decided that a piece of meat below a certain critical diameter was not a Piece of Meat in the legal sense, and it could be ingested on Fridays without peril to one's soul.

In an effort to get away from this Vonnegutesque scenario, Vatican II changed the rule to a recommendation: on Fridays, perform some act of self-denial or charity in honor of our Lord's death. This is a very sensible and adult statement, but unfortunately it came at the end of centuries in which the hierarchy had kept the laity immature by telling them what to do. People continued to take the *recommendation* (a vision of what might be) as a *rule* (the essential minimum) and it seemed to them that now there was nothing special one had to do on Fridays, so they did nothing special, and any sense of Fridayness vanished.

A similar fate has overtaken many other rules which have been changed to recommendations. We are still asking, "How little can I get away with?" As this little becomes less, everything about the Church becomes flat and tasteless—or, on the other hand, zany attempts are made to spice things up with campy pizzazz, in what has been called the Vegas Syndrome.

Legal minimalism has not gone unchallenged. In fact, one of the things we mean by "mysticism" (a strange word which yet does seem to mean something) is a direct contact with the living God who inspires us to do all sorts of heroic and good things by the very attractiveness of his presence. Laws, in such a condition, are unnecessary, for the mystic observes them "naturally, as if by habit," as St. Benedict says. "Love God and do what you like," said St. Augustine. And if what we like is not what God likes, it is clear we do not love God enough.

One way of interpreting the present religious situation is to say that it is a rebirth of mysticism. As a teacher of religion at a major university, I am struck by the increasing number of students who demand information on how to meditate. Whether it is Zen, Yoga, Native American, or Catholic does not seem to matter, so long as it leads away from the dullness of minimalist routine into personal experience of the Whatever. If this attitude can be encouraged, we will mature enough so that we can understand the force of recommendations rather than rules. I write this book as such an encouragement. By learning how to meditate at Mass, we put back together the divorced elements of practice and theory, we recover the Mystery, we contact the Center experientially, and so we go to Mass out of the expansion of love rather than the contraction of law.

Setting out for Mass, then, is, for the person who realizes the cosmic centrality of it, a matter of desire and premeditation, like going on vacation. Before going, you will want to be sure that you have some money, so you can pay your way, and you will want to look at the guidebook. The guidebook is the Missal.

The main purpose of the pre-Vatican II Missal was to give the congregation something to do that would bear a family resemblance to what the priest was doing—we followed printed words in English while the priest muttered words in Latin, and if we were clever we were able to keep up. Today, however, when the Mass texts present us with a daunting array of options which, like a shelfful of dogfood, contains little actual variety, taking a hand Missal to church is only recommended to those fortunate mutants who have an extra pair of hands to cope with both its own vagaries and the supplemental paper chase provided by the well-meaning Liturgy Committee. Its main purpose now is for preparation.

The night before Mass, or at any rate some time before

leaving the house, read through the texts in a calm, receptive manner. Let them speak to you if they will. If they do not speak, don't worry. They will have had an unnoticed effect at a subconscious level. As Buddhists say, they will have turned your karmic stream in a positive direction. You may see a theme running through the readings, particularly on major feasts. On many Sundays, a theme is not so clear, but occasionally some old text will spring out at you in a new and unexpected way, like a bite from a friendly dog.

I was brought up to say certain set prayers called Preparation for Mass. My new Missal still gives a few of these. They are rather wordy and have a lot in them about blood. If you find any of them helpful, use them, but remember it is your attitude and motivation that are important. An Anglican Bishop (the sort who is addressed as "My Lord") was visiting a farm in England. He asked the young son how he prepared for Holy Communion. "I cleans me boots, m'Lud," came the entirely satisfactory reply.

Now you are ready to go. As you cross your threshold, remember (or say out loud, if you know people won't mind) a suitable phrase such as one of the following, which I give in my own somewhat interpretative translation, to help focus your mind on what you are about to do:

"I was glad at their invitation to me, 'Let us go to the House of Yahweh.'" (Psalm 122:1)

"I lift up my eyes to God, whose throne is in the heavens." (Psalm 123:1)

"I will go to the altar of God, to God my joy." (Psalm 43:4)

"The journey of life is too great for me. I will eat and drink of Christ, and walk in the strength of that Food up to the Mount of God." (cf. I Kings 19:8)

B. ENTERING THE MANDALA

The word mandala has entered the English language, but with a very vague meaning. Partly because of Jung, who saw

mandalas but had no one to tell him how to interpret them,
any two-dimensional quaternity (a figure with four symmetrical segments) especially if enclosed in or enclosing a circle, is
called a mandala. In Buddhism, the meaning is quite precise:
a mandala means a location, a universe, and a palace.

Location   As a location, mandala refers specifically to the *bodhi-
maṇḍala*, the spot in northeastern India on which the Buddha was enlightened. This goes into Japanese as *dōjō* and is
used for the exercise hall in the martial arts. The spot on
which the exercitant moves is identified with the spot on
which the Buddha did not move. For the Christian, this
usage of mandala refers to the room in which Jesus celebrated the Last Supper, technically called the Cenacle (Supper-
Room), and then to a church or any location where Mass is
being said, which is mystically identified with the Cenacle.

Universe   In a broader sense, mandala means a universe or world-
system. Buddhists traditionally regard the earth as one
among four (or twelve) continents in a huge ocean surround-
ing an enormous mountain called Meru, with the entire system ringed by a circle of mountains and founded upon space.
That is to say, as a *cosmos* or ordered whole. They then
speak of thousands, or even an infinity, of such mandalas as
making up the entire universe. A Christian offers such a mandala, as we shall see, with the bread and wine at Mass.

Palace   Thirdly, mandala means a palace, specifically the palace of
a deity. It is in this sense which, with considerable distortion,
it has entered English. The deity lives at the center of his palace, behind a series of guarded doors. When the plan of his
palace is laid out in two dimensions, it becomes a quaternity,
but if one has learned the artistic conventions, it is easy to see
it as a three-dimensional structure. The Palace Mandala is
found in the Bible, especially the books of Ezekiel and Revelation, and St. Teresa of Avila uses the model in her *Interior
Castle*.

Everyone likes the book of Ezekiel because of chapter 1,
which gives an account of a very strange vehicle on which

God came to visit him. In Judaism, this is the basis of Merka-
bah (Chariot) Mysticism. Disciples of *Chariots of the Gods*
are convinced that this is one of "those" chariots. Encouraged by such a splendid opening, people may read on, hop-
ing for more of the same. Chapter 40 usually brings them to a
halt. From there to the end (chapter 48) it is a description of
the new Temple which is to be built. An angel appears and
conducts Ezekiel on a tour of the visionary mock-up of the
Temple, pointing out such details as the following:

> Then he brought me to the vestibule of the temple and
> measured the jambs of the vestibule, five cubits on either
> side; and the breadth of the gate was fourteen cubits; and the
> sidewalls of the gate were three cubits on either side. The
> length of the vestibule was twenty cubits, and the breadth
> twelve cubits; and ten steps led up to it; and there were pillars
> beside the jambs on either side.
>
> (*Ezekiel 40:48-49; RSV*)

How could it possibly matter to a Christian today that in a
vision of a Jewish temple that was not, in the event, built, one
of the vestibules was twenty cubits (about 35 feet) long? After
learning about the Liturgy of the Mandala it occurred to me
that the precise details do not matter, but it matters very
much that the details are precise.

A Palace Mandala has nothing haphazard about it. It is an
instrument of enlightenment and if it is improperly put together it will not work. Tibetan monks study for years under a
qualified teacher before they are allowed to construct one.
There is a curious belief among many Western Buddhist sym-
pathizers that one may attain enlightenment quickly by getting high occasionally on some formless sitting. But traveling
toward nirvana requires at least as much effort and precision
as traveling to the moon. And if a Christian thinks that effort
and precision are not needed to go to God, he or she falls into a belief in the TV Dinner God, with all the doleful conse-
quences I have mentioned. So, in Bible reading, Ezekiel

40-48 should definitely not be skipped. It should be read as
carefully as the "interesting" parts. Build up, in your imagination, the visionary Temple piece by piece, as if you were Ezekiel constructing a Palace Mandala for God under the gui-
dance of his angelic guru. You may not get everything clearly
(I tend to get my vestibules muddled), but you will have the
sense of participating in the vital process of preparing a worthy house for the Lord of All.

If you do this, then Revelation 21-22 will make sense as
the logical next step in understanding the Christian mandala.
These culminating passages of the New Testament describe
the end of this world order and its replacement by a new
order which is beyond time (therefore it has no sun or moon
—Revelation 21:23). A New Jerusalem descends from
heaven, like *Close Encounters of the Third Kind*, but consid-
erably more alive than that mechanical apocalypse. The imagery is based largely on Ezekiel's Temple, although the New
Jerusalem does not have a temple because the distinction between sacred and secular is therein transcended.

The New Jerusalem is as much like a mandala as anything
in a Buddhist text. It is set upon and made up of jewels, and it
glows with their rainbow light. It is perfectly symmetrical, being a cube fifteen hundred miles broad, long, and high. It has
twelve symmetrically placed gates, each of which is an enormous single pearl which, as if it had been thought up by Isaac
Asimov, is a solid-but-not-solid transducer between the timelessness inside and time outside. It illuminates the universe
and purifies anyone who enters it. It contains the cosmic tree
which constantly bears curative leaves and different kinds of
fruit adapted to all conditions, and from it there flows a crystal
stream of the water of life.

Artists have regrettably trivialized this by making it look like
a real city. The Hollywood cliché of the Pearly Gates, suspi-
ciously resembling those of Universal Studios, is the worst example of such nonsense. As a Palace Mandala, the New Jerusalem is quite unlike any physical city. It is not just a nice

place for one's cosmic retirement, a Sun City, Arizona, in the sky; it is the timeless and placeless City of God in which we, as Christians, are already living, but do not realize it. When we go to Mass, we re-activate our knowledge that this is where we are.

St. Teresa's *Interior Castle* is a remarkable adaptation of the Buddhist Tantric ritual of entry into the Palace Mandala. Except that there is no evidence that she ever took a course in the Buddhist Tantras. As a person who prayed earnestly for the conversion of Protestants to Christ, the Mystical Doctor of Ávila would no doubt have beaten me severely over the head with the tambourine she used for dancing with her nuns during free time, had I suggested such a course to her. So it is still more remarkable. The resemblances get Jungians very excited and they start murmuring about archetypes, but, at least for now, I would prefer to let sleeping archetypes lie and just look at what we have.

The Interior Castle, now available in a new, fresh translation by Kieran Kavanaugh and Otilio Rodriguez (New York: Paulist Press, 1979), may have come to Teresa in a vision. A historically suspect account supposedly given to her confessor says that she saw "a most beautiful crystal globe like a castle in which she saw seven dwelling places, and in the seventh, which was in the center, the King of Glory dwelt in the greatest splendor. From there he beautified and illumined all those dwelling places to the outer wall. The inhabitants received more light the nearer they were to the center. Outside the castle all was darkness, with toads, vipers, and other poisonous vermin . . ." (quoted in Ibid., p. 20).

This spherical, jewellike castle has seven "dwelling places" or sets of rooms, progressively nearer the core. In the outer ones dwell Christians who concentrate on good works and spiritual reading, but who do not have a deep, interior knowledge of God. Further in are the rooms where union with God and the soul takes place, and silence supercedes speech and thought. The innermost room is the scene of union with the divinized humanity of Christ, which allows the Christian to participate fully in the busyness and pressure of everyday living without losing a profound sense of inner peace, for she now lives in the Trinity and the Trinity in her.

This is a full and rather precise account of a Christian Palace Mandala. A Buddhist Palace Mandala is four-square on the outside, and its gates are guarded by fierce, flaming deities called Compassion Kings because they compassionately destroy the defilements of those who enter. Inside, it is circular, often it is a conical mountain, and as the practitioner advances up the mountain in his imagination, he is more and more purified and his mind shines out with Original Buddha Nature. At the top, or center, he meets the Entity (a deity, Bodhisattva or Buddha) and merges with him or her. Since that Entity is a good Mahāyāna Buddhist, he or she is simultaneously out of saṃsāra and involved in saṃsāra. Thus, the practitioner begins to act in the busyness of the worlds for the good of all beings, while remaining calmly rooted in Emptiness.

These three mandalas—location, universe, and palace— are not entirely distinct from each other. The Palace Mandala is the most obvious liturgical mandala, since we enter into it in the form of the church building. But it is also, for the Christian, the mystical re-presentation of the Cenacle, that is, of the Location Mandala. At the Offertory, priest and people offer the universe to God as a Buddhist offers a Universe Mandala to the Buddhas or to his Teacher. In Holy Communion, this universe is received back from God transfigured into the New Jerusalem, in which the Christian henceforth tries to live.

It has taken some time to explain what a mandala is. But now that we know, let us step into St. Malachy's and see what happens if we regard it as a Palace and Location Mandala.

We should note that preparations have been made before we arrived, as they are also made beforehand by an initiating lama. It is not trivial to observe that there is a building. A great deal of work went into putting it up, and its arrangement is not haphazard. The focus of the church is the altar, which may be in the center or at the far end. The rest of the building is no more than a house for the protection of the altar. It is the heart of the mandala. Often there is a Tabernacle containing the Sacrament, but it was a mistake which Vatican II corrected to regard the Tabernacle as the heart. Without the altar, on which the consecration takes place, the Tabernacle would be merely a fancy bread box. The altar is surrounded by, or at the end of, a series of "rooms." Its own room is called the Sanctuary (Sacred Place), and no one goes in there during Mass who does not have a direct role to play in the central liturgical action. (Of course, the aforementioned leotarded Californian invited everyone in to be chummy, but in so doing he announced his incomprehension of the transformative purpose of liturgy.) At the outer edge of the Sanctuary is the pulpit and/or lectern, from where the Heart speaks to us, like the deity coming out of his mandala to give us a lecture before allowing us in. (I must say I found that this aspect of the Mandala Liturgy reminded me a little of a grumpy schoolmaster, but perhaps that is not inappropriate.)

Next out from the Sanctuary is the Nave, so called because it resembles, in Gothic cathedrals, an upside-down ship (Latin *navis*, hence English "navy"), in which the congregation sits. Cathedrals and monastic churches may have an intermediate room between the Sanctuary and the Nave called the Choir, where the monks or choristers sit to sing the music. The entrance to the church, called the Narthex or Porch, is the outermost room and it usually has doors leading both into the Nave and out into the street. This is a kind of spiritual decompression chamber for passing into and out of the mandala, the Pearl-Gate of the New Jerusalem. It often contains a subroom called the Baptistery which holds the

Font, since Baptism is the rite of initiation into the Church. A properly designed Baptistery will be at a lower level than the Porch, to symbolize going down into and coming up out of the river of Baptism.

On the outside walls of the Nave there will usually be one or more Confessionals or Rooms of Reconciliation, where those who have made themselves too impure to enter safely into the heart of the mandala may receive the purification of absolution. The entire building was sealed off to undesirable spiritual forces by the Bishop when he consecrated the church by saying special blessings at various points along the inside of the outer walls. These points are generally marked by consecration crosses and candle sconces. The preparations have been completed by the setting up of the Sanctuary for the liturgical action just before the arrival of the congregation.

As you enter the Porch, you have time to remember that you are not entering just any building, you are entering a mandala. As you pass from the Porch to the Nave, there should be a Holy Water Stoup. Crossing yourself with Holy Water is a sacramental, rather than a sacrament. A sacrament, such as Baptism, is effective on its own account, and all we do is appropriate the gift. A sacramental has a kind of potentiality which does not come alive unless we activate it by an awareness (or "by faith," whatever that means) of what we are doing and what we wish it to do. Taking Holy Water is a special Catholic form of the ritual bath which so many religions require before one enters into the holy place. If there is no Holy Water Stoup, as there may not be if your priest is very Relevant, cross yourself anyhow and imagine the Holy Water.

Before taking your seat, it is customary to reverence the altar, that is, to acknowledge the sacred focus of the mandala. The tradition has grown up of doing this by a genuflection, although a dignified bow is really quite sufficient. The reverence is necessary because of our entering status as Servant.

It is appropriate to remain kneeling for some time before Mass begins, in order to maintain the awareness of Servant status. Private prayer at this time should be concerned with what Buddhists call Correcting Motivation. Ask yourself, "Why am I here? Fear of punishment if I don't show? Custom? Hopes of meeting that certain man or woman and making a date? Desire to escape the world and go to heaven?" All these are trivial reasons. The only real reason for going to Mass is to worship God in such a way that it results in better service of other creatures. When your motivation has come around to this, you are ready to begin Mass.

C. I AM SPEECH

The Mass is divided into two main parts: Word and Sacrament. The first is verbal, the second is nonverbal and leads to an intimate communion between the soul and God. The Logos comes to us first as Speech and then as Food. The progression is very much like that to the center of St. Teresa's castle. It is also like getting to know a friend, or falling in love. At first the communication is verbal. Then words become inadequate, there is touching, union, and silence. Sexual imagery has been used by many of the great Christian mystics to illustrate their experiences, and the highest union is called the Spiritual Marriage. Similar ideas are found in Tantra and in the worship of the Hindu god Krishna. A Christian does not leave her sexual feelings at the door of the mandala, although actual orgies are not called for, even by the California gentleman in leotards.

But before you get too aroused, I must return to the first part of the Mass, where speech is the main vehicle of communication.

1. INTRODUCTORY RITES:
THE STATUS OF SERVANT

The priest enters and greets the people with a short formula such as "The Lord be with you," to which we respond, "And also with you." This is a simple interchange of great power. Priest and people unite themselves in the one God, who is equally with all, from the very beginning of the ceremony. Within the Church there are differences of function, but we are all alike in God's love. The words of the exchange are of great antiquity, and they are general rather than particular. Antiquity and generality cover the surface ego of the priest like his chasuble and remind us of the catholicity (the universality) of the Church. A priest who, at this solemn moment which links together all the Christians of the past, present, and future, volunteers his personal name and insists that we all turn to our neighbor and do likewise, has allowed his surface ego to overpower his sense of catholicity, of the solid corporality of the Church, and deserves therefore to be hung by his toenails and beaten with a wet fish until he relents.

Then the priest sprinkles the people with Holy Water, reinforcing the symbolism of the Stoup at the door. Or rather, as the rubrics say, he "may" do this. Devoured by legal minimalism, most priests do not do it. This is a great pity, for the prayers that go with the ceremony are very much to the point in reminding us that, as we and our planet are mostly water, and we were born wet and sticky in the biological mode, so water is vital to our birth and continued spiritual health. Read the prayers and see what you are missing. The mixing of salt and water, which is another "may," goes back to the time, not so long ago, when there was no refrigeration, and salt was the only preservative, thus it "preserves" us from evil. Notice the text adapted from Ezekiel 47, which will now be meaningful.

When the Sprinkling is omitted, the Penitential Rite is used. This is very appropriate for weekdays, and Sundays in

Advent and Lent, but it is a little grim for normal Sundays, which are supposed to be mini-Easters. It does, however, underline our preliminary Servant status, with examination of conscience, confession, absolution, and Kyrie.

Kyrie means "Lord!" in Greek—it is in the Vocative Case, addressing him. It is a very ancient part of the Mass, originating from the days when even the Pope said Mass in Greek, because that was the international language of the time. The Roman Mass was put into Latin when people no longer understood Greek. The Kyrie was, and still is in the Greek Orthodox Church, a prominent part of the liturgy. The priest makes many petitions and to each of them the choir responds Kyrie eleison, "Lord, have mercy." Nicholas Cabasilas says that this is the only prayer of which we are worthy. At the level of Servant, this is true. The Kyrie has been severely reduced in successive revisions of the Roman Mass, until now it is as prominent as the vermiform appendix and, like it, is usually cut out.

The Kyrie is addressed three times to the Father (Kyrie eleison), three times to the Son (Christe eleison), and three times to the Spirit (Kyrie eleison again). It is theologically balanced, for it realizes that a Christian does not pray to one Person at a time, but to the entire Trinity. The eight alternatives provided in the new Missal address Christ alone, and thus, if they are not actually heretical, they are certainly very misleading. Subsequent revisions should restore the Trinitarian balance.

Having received preliminary purification, on Sundays and Feasts except during Advent and Lent the door to heaven opens and we sing the Gloria. This is the first vision in the Mass, and in order to see it we need to forget about how St. Malachy's looks, and practice Visualization. Visualization is an ancient Tantric practice that sounds very modern. Psychologists would call it projection.

Projection is unhealthy only when it is not under a person's control. Some Western physicians have recently discovered that certain cures seem to be effected by the patient's projecting healing visualizations. This therapy has been used by Tibetan doctors for about fifteen hundred years. Meditative visualization of religious subjects helps to transform the consciousness so that we act in accordance with what we see. It is always, unless something goes wrong, under the meditator's control.

Catholicism has traditionally classified meditative visions into two: imaginary and intellectual. These terms are taken directly from the Latin, where they make sense, and put into English, where they are nonsense. Imaginary means "with an image." Intellectual means "in the *intellectus*," the *intellectus* being a very deep level of the mind that has nothing to do with the surface level indicated by the English word *intellect*. I would like to rename them Pictorial and Emotive. An Emotive Vision comes later than a Pictorial Vision and is more profound than it.

When you meet people for the first time, appearances count for everything, for you have no other way of judging them. If you meet them often, and become good friends, their personality begins to have more importance than their looks or habits of dressing. Try thinking of a good friend, preferably one you have known for a long time and with whom there is no sexual involvement. What comes to mind? Probably nothing very visual. You do not see them in the room but you *feel as if* they were in the room. That is an Emotive Vision.

If you were to have a Pictorial Vision of St. Joseph picking out some lumber at the timber yard, or of our Lady selecting babyfood in the supermarket, you would not know it was a vision until they came over and introduced themselves. And even then you could not be sure that you were not going crazy, or talking to someone who was crazy. The Church has always been very suspicious of Pictorial Visions. It has said that they could easily be hallucinations produced by the Devil. Even if they come from God, the Church recommends that we ignore them, for they have shape and God is formless. Therefore, an Emotive Vision, which is formless, is more likely to be divine in origin. Whether it is or not is determined by its fruits: if a vision leads to pride and hatred, it is demonic; conversely, if it leads to humility and compassion, it is divine.

The practice of meditative visualization begins with projecting a Pictorial Vision, and as quickly as possible it dispenses with the picture and moves on to an Emotive Vision. The Pictorial Vision should be as detailed as you can make it, but if it keeps going fuzzy, there is nothing to worry about. You are only constructing a meditative aid, not a real entity. You should always be aware that you are projecting, and you should always feel in complete control of the image. If you have repeated trouble with either of these aspects of visualization, you need to check with a qualified meditation teacher whom you can trust, preferably a Tibetan lama, of whom there are now quite a number in America.

As the Gloria proceeds, visualize, either pictorially or emotively, God the Father as a King seated on a magnificent throne in front and slightly above you. God the Son sits to his right, and God the Holy Spirit to his left. Each Person has the same features (since God transcends gender, "his" features are best visualized as androgynous) but wears different robes: pale pastels for the Father, who really is invisible behind a wall of light, royal purple for the Son, and the green of nature for the Spirit. You may add as many angels as you can fit.

The priest then says the Opening Prayer, which we used to call the Collect because it collects together the individual prayers of the people. It is introduced by a general invitation, "Let us pray for such-and-such." There is a pause (this pause is very important—priests who omit it are not letting the laypeople participate fully) during which you can pray silently for such-and-such in your own words, and then the priest says the formal, printed words, collecting up our private prayers. Try to hold the visualization throughout the Prayer, so that you know in whose presence you are praying.

At the end of the Prayer, dissolve the visualization into light, or make it rise through the ceiling, and dismiss it. Like any tool, it has fulfilled its purpose and may be laid aside. If you cannot dismiss the visualization easily, you are not controlling it and need to seek help.

This is the end of the state where the status of Servant is maintained. We now move in closer, as Friends.

2. LITURGY OF THE WORD:
   THE STATUS OF FRIEND

(a) The Readings: Myth makes Sense
Reading the Bible is not like reading the newspaper. We read a newspaper to get information about what is happening in ordinary space-time, and we read it in an active mode. The Bible speaks to us from nonordinary reality, and we receive its message passively, as if digesting food. The material of the Bible is called *myth*. In ordinary language, myth means something which is not true, but to the scholar of religions it means something which is *more true* than the information of ordinary space-time, because it gives meaning to it.

The story of Adam and Eve is a myth. The events in the story did not happen, but they are true. We are all Adams and Eves, that is to say, we were all intended by God to be his companions, his co-workers on this planet, but we have all gone wrong by trying to take over in our own right. The book of Genesis tells us this in the form of a story which happened long ago. As we say in fairy tales, it happened "once upon a time." Children know quite well that "once upon a time" cannot be dated on the calendar. It means "once in nonordinary reality." For ordinary reality this "once" is both "never" and "always." As we grow up, we lose this sense of a timeless nonordinary reality, demand that everything be dated, find that Adam and Eve cannot be dated, and reject the biblical story as pure fantasy.

What we are doing is making a distinction between Myth and History, and allowing only History as evidence. This is a fairly new distinction, perhaps not more than three hundred years old. For thousands of years before that, there was a sense of "what happened," and its truth or falsity was judged in respect of how things seemed to be at the time that "what happened" was being worked out. Because we seemed to have "fallen from grace," it was regarded as certain that such a falling was "what happened." This led to pseudohistories of the Fallen Race, all very precisely dated, and an account of a Restoration in Christ at a certain date.

The Time of Christ is ordinary time. He can be dated. But his actions are timeless, like those of Adam and Eve. In Christ we see the intersection of timeless Myth with timeable History. Occasionally this intersection is difficult to plot, but that is a technical matter which we can leave to the biblical scholars. Whether or not Jesus did or said a certain thing is not as important, to the ordinary Christian, as the knowledge that Jesus existed in History and, *historico-mythologically*, did or said what is recorded of him. The miracles, for example, may or may not have been historical. (We cannot say that they were not—similar miracles are reported from India all the time.) But Christ is the historical doorway to a mythological reality in which the miracles are true. Biblical scholars do not seem to understand this, perhaps because they regard myth as the proper subject matter of historians of religion, and then assume that the history of religions, like adultery, is never done at home—we do it only to the pagans. Hence they apply their considerable intellects to the nonproblem of sorting History from Myth in a definitive way and, after producing lengthy treatises on the topic in ponderous German prose, confess that they are not getting anywhere. But from the perspective of History-Myth, it is quite clear: we are all Adams and Eves who are always perfect, always falling, and always being redeemed in the timeless time of Christ.

Jungian psychologists distinguish Myth from History by saying that History is an external event and Myth is an internal event. This is a helpful idea which we may use to restore our faith in Myth if we cannot see it as anything but fiction. But it violates its sources, for it separates subject (Myth) from object (History), whereas the whole point of the ancient idea of "what happened" is that this distinction was not made.

The Bible, then, gives us the Myth of the Christian experience, which occasionally, in both the Old and New Testaments, intersects with History. This Myth is called Salvation History (a really terrible term, but it was made up by the Germans—Heilsgeschichte—and I cannot do anything about it). It tells how, in the providence of God, we come to be where we are. This kind of literature has been with the human race for as long as we know. The people ask, "Why is the sun hot?" and the elders tell the traditional story about it. This is an excellent attitude for us to have at Mass. We ask, "Who is Christ?" and we sit around the campfire while the Bible tells us the answer.

Sometimes the ancient myths are acted out by certain members of the tribe. The acting out of the Christian Myth is fairly clear in Orthodox liturgies, but it has become obscured in the Catholic Mass. In Orthodoxy, the bread and wine are prepared beforehand behind closed doors, signifying the secrecy of Christ's early life and his hiddenness in the Old Testament. Then, the priest and acolytes enter the nave from the door on the proper right of the Sanctuary (an Orthodox church walls off the mandalic focus rather completely) on two occasions. The first is called the Minor Entrance, when the Book of the Gospels is brought in and carried round and back to the altar, symbolizing the teaching ministry of Christ. The second, the Major Entrance, introduces the bread and wine in a symbol of Christ's going up to Jerusalem to be sacrificed. Reaching the altar, the priest consecrates the elements, marking Christ's death, and distributes them in Holy Communion, marking his Resurrection.

We see some of this in the Roman Mass, but the progression is different, and its clarity is mostly restricted to the Readings. On Sundays and feasts, there are three readings and two responses. The first reading is from the Old Testament, the second from the non-Gospel part of the New Testament, and the third from the Gospels. The movement is from Old Testament prophecy about Christ, through New Testament proclamation about Christ, to the words of Christ himself (the historico-mythologically true words, of course!). There is an exception: during the Easter season, the Church is so pleased to report the Resurrection that she gives no time at all to reading the Old Testament. On weekdays, also, there are only two readings, for the sake of time, and the story of Salvation History is compressed.

While listening to the readings, you may appropriately adopt the status of a Friend of God. You are no longer overwhelmed by God's glory and your own sinfulness, you have been asked into the community of his friends and are being told stories about his secret workings on behalf of all creation.

After the Old Testament reading we sing an Old Testament hymn, called a *psalm*, with a suitable response sung as a refrain after each verse. (Lectors/Cantors, please note: this is called a Responsorial Psalm because it is a Psalm with a Response. It is incomprehensible to announce the Response by saying "The Responsorial Psalm is . . . .") This leads us naturally into the New Testament reading. The Gospel reading follows, and since it centers on the words of the Godman, several things are done to honor it. It is read by the priest, whose special function at Mass is to act out the role of Christ; acclamations of joy and praise come before and after it; and we all stand up as we would do if someone of importance, like the President of the United States, were to enter the room.

It has also become traditional for everyone to make the

sign of the Cross with their right thumb on their forehead, lips, and breast as the Gospel reading is announced. This reminds me of two things. In Buddhism, the forehead, throat, and heart are said to be the centers of the body, speech, and mind (Buddhists think with their hearts, which is a very integrated way to think) and the seed-mantras OṂ, ĀḤ, and HŪṂ are said to reside there. This is not quite the same as the Catholic tradition, but it resonates interestingly with it. The second thing it reminds me of is that Christ, as the Word Incarnate, is therefore Wisdom Incarnate. Wisdom is symbolized in many religions by a sword. Hebrews 4:12 compares the Word of God to a two-edged sword dividing truth from falsehood. By making the Cross on ourselves in these three places we draw the Incarnate Sword down through our bodies, like lightning piercing the clouds of ignorance, and prepare ourselves to hear the words of Widsom himself. In the Orthodox Liturgy, the Deacon holds the Book of the Gospels high and chants, "Wisdom! Let us listen!"

WISDOM SPEAKS

Philosophy
is come among us;
striding confidently
into death.

When the priest finishes the Gospel, he kisses the text and says "May the words of the Gospel wipe away our sins." This sentence, which I was glad to see was not relevanced away in the new Missal, harks back to wisdom as a mantra. Mantras are sounds which, like music, have a psychological effect even through they may not have a dictionary meaning. Mantras can destroy bad karma just by being said. When the words of the Gospel are regarded as wiping away sins, they are being used as mantras. Some mantras have a dictionary meaning in addition to their inherent effectiveness. The words of the Gospel, the words of Wisdom Incarnate, are

mantras with meaning. You should try to follow their meaning, but even if you cannot understand them, they will have a
beneficial effect on your deep consciousness. The story is
told of a frog who was accidentally crushed during a sermon
being given by the Buddha. Immediately he was reborn as a
god. Startled, he looked for the reason, and found that it was
due to the mantric effect of the Buddha's words, even
though, having been a frog, he had not understood them.

The Gospel reading over, we sit down and, with an inward
groan, await the Homily.

(b) The Homily: How to make the Best of It

There is no doubt that for the most of us the Homily, or
Sermon, is the low point of the Mass. It seems to be a problem for the priest also. He has to say something, and he is
supposed to say something that relates to the Mass of the
day, especially to the Gospel text, but he has been out of the
seminary for years, he has had no time to keep up on his
reading, he has had a lot of sick calls this week, and he has
just found out that the rectory has dry rot, the Youth Group
dance ended with suspicious goings-on in the dark, his
housekeeper is quitting, and the Bishop has increased the fi-
nancial quota his parish is supposed to give to the diocese.
All he has time for is something thrown together or copied
from a book of sermons. And on Trinity Sunday, that fearful
day when he must try to explain the highest mystery of the
Christian faith, his courage fails him and he talks about the
budget instead.

Why do we put ourselves through this? The Orthodox do
not. The sermon comes at the end of the Liturgy, after a brief
pause during which those who have had enough may leave.
In Orthodoxy, again, the Liturgy is the primary teacher. If
you are paying attention, the whole thing is a sermon. However, the Mass puts it where it is, and we have to make the
best of it.

The sermon is supposed to gather up the myth in the readings and bring it into space-time, applying it to a particular congregation at a particular moment in history. There is a problem in that most congregations outside of monasteries and university campuses are made up of people of very widely varying ages, mentalities, backgrounds, and outlooks. An effective sermon can, at best, hit this random sampling in the middle of its Bell curve. A good way for it to do this is for it to make only one basic point. If time permits, and the congregation doesn't seem too dazed or fidgety, the priest might want to elaborate on this point, but if too many points are brought in, the young and less intelligent get lost, whereas if there is no solid point, the older and more intelligent become frustrated and feel they are wasting their time. A short, snappy sermon that makes one point and, following the excellent advice given to Alice, begins at the beginning, goes on to the end, and there stops, should not take more than a few minutes to prepare in note form, and the congregation will be left feeling that it has been given something on which it can reflect.

If you as a layperson find yourself trapped by a long, rambling sermon that is making no sense, try to pick out one salient point of value. I find I can usually squeeze one out even when it isn't really there. Then think about that for the rest of the sermon, ignoring the remainder of what the priest says. In extreme cases, I have followed the advice of Erasmus, who said that if the sermon were not edifying, one should read an improving book. For refreshment, it is good to go on occasion to a vital monastery and hear a sermon which the man has had time to prepare. The best preparation for a sermon is not done the night before by glancing through the texts: it grows as a natural consequence out of a life dedicated to prayer. Most parish priests quite legitimately do not have time for such preparation. They should therefore say less and not try for a profundity which they do not have.

(c) *The Creed: A Curious Check-List*

After the Homily there is a great yawning and struggling and wondering what to do with the baby, and we all stand up and recite a piece of the most high-flown philosophy ever written, called the Nicene Creed. At a meeting of professors of medieval philosophy, such a procedure might seem natural, but as a standard exercise imposed upon ordinary people, it is quite curious. I myself am not sure what it means, though I have studied it in its original Greek.

Of all religions, Christianity is the most concerned, even obsessed, with right belief, that is, "orthodoxy." Other religions put more emphasis on "orthopraxy," or right activity. There was once a famous meeting of Jews to put God on trial for the Holocaust. Had God acted rightly? The most learned rabbis discussed the topic for two or three days straight, and finally brought in their verdict. God was guilty. A Christian under such circumstances would have given up his religion (or "renounced his *faith*," as we significantly put it). The Jews, however, next announced, "And now it is time for prayer." A Jew is a Jew because of what he is and does, not because of what he believes.

A Christian, on the other hand, tends to define himself more by what he believes. Many even identify all religion with belief. "I'm not religious," people often tell me, "I don't believe anything." I reply that belief is peripheral in most religions. Why is it so important in Christianity? There does not seem to be a really good answer to this, but I can give you my suspicions.

The first Christians had a very simple Creed. When the pagans shouted "Caesar is Lord," the Christians would retaliate with "Christ is Lord." That would seem to be about enough. Islam, by no means a vague affair, requires the Muslim to believe only that God is One and that Muḥammad is his Messenger. The other four basic requirements of the religion are orthopraxy—prayer, almsgiving, fasting, pilgrimage. Elaborate theologies can be studied later, if one wishes, but this simple belief is enough for entrance into full membership.

In Christianity, the problem came up, "Who is Christ?" and instead of answering by *actions*, as Christ himself had done, the Church turned the matter over to the philosophers, who came up with theories as elaborate and generally unintelligible as the babblings of the Philosopher in *The Yellow Submarine*. The theories were then adopted by the hierarchy as a test of who was in the Church and who was not. This was very convenient for the hierarchy, for it allowed it to count noses, find out how it was doing on converts, and estimate its income. All Christian groups seem to be united in this activity. The Vatican can tell instantly how many Catholics there are supposed to be, and only the other night a Protestant gentleman with a voice as loud as his tie announced over the television that two more souls had just been saved in Durham, North Carolina. Significant groups of laypeople, however, have, throughout the history of the Church, troubled the hierarchy by reacting against this overintellectual, elitist, almost Gnostic position. Today I hear so many people saying "I can't believe all that stuff" and "What does it matter, anyway?" When I tell them I am not sure if *I* believe all that stuff, they reply, "Then you can't be a Christian."

But what is a Christian? A Christian is a follower of Christ. Christ is found, subsequent to his Resurrection, in the Church. The Church is the guardian of the traditions about Christ (the Bible) and of Christ's continuing organic life on earth, because of which she is called the Mystical Body of Christ and as which she dispenses the sacraments.

The sacraments are the heart of the matter. If I meet someone, I do not know anything about them except how they look and how their personality begins to come across. Subsequently, I learn more about how they think and about their hopes and fears. So it is with Christ. First we have to meet him, organically, physically, through the water of Baptism and the bread and wine of the Mass which his Mystical Body wears in place of the skin which his fleshly body wore. Then slowly, we learn more about him and his will for us and for all his creation.

Many people today hunger for this immediate contact with Christ, but when they come to the Catholic Church, they meet a forbidding wall of dogma, and they turn to various charismatic and revivalist groups of Christians whom we collectively call Jesus Freaks or Born-Again Christians. There they are told that a true Christian is not one who believes propositions One through Umpteen, but one who has found (or has been found by) Christ, and knows him. I do not see how anyone could dispute this. Without Christ, it is difficult to understand what Christianity could possibly be all about.

I have attended meetings of some of these groups and I appreciate and respect their sincerity. But I have a problem with them. They seem to me to make an excellent beginning but not to go anywhere. After getting born again, all you can do is try to convince others to join and watch them get born again with the weepy satisfaction of a mother who remembers her own wedding as she marries her daughter off. Put another way, these people *meet* Christ but they never seem to get to *know* him. They are always in the ecstasy of having just fallen in love, but they do not mature into matrimony. Beside the great mystics of Catholicism and Orthodoxy, they are children. Intensely living children indeed, but still children.

In Buddhist terms, there is no Way (*mārga*), no Spiritual Path, no entry into the deeper and deeper recesses of the mandala nor ascent to the higher and higher slopes of the Mountain.

St. Thomas Aquinas said that philosophy was the handmaiden of theology. If we take this remark to its logical conclusion, it amounts to saying that all *theory about Christ* is subservient to all *experience of Christ*. Now, let it be carefully noted that this is not to say that *every* experience of Christ is dominant over *any* theory about him. I may be thoroughly convinced that Mr. Jones is a cockroach. I may experience him as a cockroach and try to squash him. But the majority of people will tell me that Mr. Jones is not a cockroach, he is a human being, and if I am going to live among them, I must also somehow see him that way. That is to say, I must take the *totality* of experience over how things seem to me at the moment.

So it is with knowing Christ. Over the centuries, the Church has built up a body of experience about Christ which has stood the test of time, surviving intellectual investigation and experiential testing by the best scholars and large numbers of everyday folk who are not about to be put off with fakes. (Peasants are far from being the simpletons of romantic literature; it takes great shrewdness to live off the land.) This body of experience with the bugs worked out is called the Deposit of Faith and it is rather like the deposit in a stock pot. It has a rich and complex flavor. It is the job of the Pope and the Bishops, in collaboration with the laity, to see that no one puts a dead rat or other unsuitable item into this stock pot, but also to recognize that the addition of certain new ingredients would help the flavor. Thus, if a Moral Majority member tells me that God is opposed to the Equal Rights Amendment, or if Seth (of *Seth Speaks*) reports that Christ was only a man, and that a substitute lunatic was crucified, I recognize these statements immediately as dead rats, and I try to stop them from going into the pot. But certain features of African traditional culture, such as co-habitation before final marriage, may be just the thing to add to African Catholicism in order to bring out the truly universal flavor of the catholicity of Christ, even though they are new in terms of the Church's formal teaching.

I do not, therefore, recommend ignoring the Creed, as do many Evangelical preachers, for the Creed helps us into the deep reality of Christ after our first meeting. This, in fact, is how it came to be written, as I have already hinted. The Creed does not give us a complete systematic theology. It was developed over time as a kind of biological defense against attack. In a sense, it is scar tissue on the Mystical Body. In the early Church, the main controversies were over the Person of Christ, and therefore the Creed spends most of its time on this, affirming its own position against various other positions which it regarded as heresies, that is, as alien flavors being added to the Deposit of Faith. The Church affirmed that the Christ it knew was eternal, identical in being with the Father, truly incarnate, truly killed, now truly risen and reigning. All these views were contested at the time, and the Church found that the rival views did not mesh with the fullness of her collective experience. The Creed has a short prologue about the Father, and a grab-bag postscript. None of these items was then being seriously disputed, and they could therefore be dealt with very briefly. Today, of course, we may need to expand on them. For instance, what does "the Catholic Church" mean? All Christians who use the Creed recite these words, but all groups interpret them differently—always in their own favor, naturally enough. For discussions of these questions we must go to the theological works. It is not my purpose to explain the "what" of the Creed, still less to present an entire exposition of theology, but to speak of the "why" of the Creed in order to help you to deal with it when it comes along at Mass.

It seems to me that the most sensible way for the Christian to approach the Creeds is to repeat the process by which the Church composed them, that is, our own spiritual growth (ontogeny) should be a rapid replay of the spiritual growth of the Church's understanding of Christ (phylogeny). First one approaches Christ as a being of fascination and power, as the Disciples and Apostles apparently did—the Gospels are full of remarks to the effect that the followers of Jesus could not decide who or what he was, nor could they understand the significance of what he was doing. All that came later, most likely after the Resurrection. The decision that Christ must have been *God* is found only in the later strata of the New Testament, but the realization that he was a force to be reckoned with is very early. I believe that this preliminary response to Christ as a force to be reckoned with, as someone who gets you up out of your seat to go over and talk to him, should be enough for Baptism and admission to Holy Communion. We should not worry that the person might not "really" know what he is doing when receiving Communion: do any of us "really" understand it? The person should then take instruction in basic doctrine about the Deposit of Faith, receive the sacraments of Communion and Reconciliation regularly, be taught how to pray, meditate, and read the Bible and the mystics intelligently, and asked to report how she is doing. If nothing is meshing after a reasonable trial, it is time to leave and experiment with something else. If, however, it all seems to come naturally together, then at a certain point the person should receive the sacrament of Confirmation and advance to full membership in the Church.

This method not only has the respectability of being very ancient—so-called heretics had nearly always been baptized and had received Communion before it was decided, often long after their deaths, that their ideas were out of line—it would also be more in accord with human psychology and it would not make unreasonable demands upon us to accept elaborate theological and philosophical systems on blind faith. It would make the Church seem more accepting and loving than dogmatic and judgmental, and it would convert the Inquisition (lately renamed the Congregation on Christian Doctrine in the hopes that we might all forget its dismal past) from a schoolmaster into a body for the sympathetic investigation of new ideas.

Toward the end of his life, St. Thomas Aquinas had a vision, in comparison with which, he said, all his considerable writing on theology was like a wisp of straw. Theology is an aid to understanding the fullness of Christ, but having accepted it we must go beyond it. It is what Buddhists call *prajñapti*, "operational hypothesis."

THE END OF THE SUMMA THEOLOGICA

Beyond the solemn
puzzles of Theology
lies the transolympian
laughter of Christ.

So, say the Creed and don't worry too much about it at first, but expect that you are going to sink more and more into it, and agree with more and more of it, as you continue to study, pray, and meet Christ in his Church.

A brief note on ritual. It is recommended that we bow during the mention of the Incarnation ("by the power of the Holy Spirit he was born of the Virgin Mary and became man"), but nobody seems to do it. There used to be a *rule* that we should kneel at this point, now there is a *recommendation* to bow, so of course nobody does anything. It is very appropriate, however, to make a gesture of humility along with the account of Christ's humbling himself to our human realm. Try it. It helps recollection.

(d) Intercessions: Transferring the Merit

The Intercessions, or Prayer of the Faithful, are a bridge between the predominantly verbal and the predominantly physical (food) sections of the Mass. In Teresa's castle, they stand at the entrance to the fourth set of rooms, after which true contemplative prayer, and then the Spiritual Marriage, occurs.

It is worth noting that this is the only place in the Mass where we come up with a shopping list of things we want for ourselves and others, and hand it to God. For many people, prayer is nothing more than a shopping list. If they then do not get what they want, they decide that prayer is useless, and stop doing it. But, as we see, the shopping list is only a very small part of the quintessential prayer called the Mass. It makes sense here because we have it in a proper context. We have abased ourselves before God's glory, heard him speaking to us through the Bible, and are about to meet him in the silence of Communion. Just before that intimate meeting, we ask him, as his friends, for what we think will be truly beneficial for ourselves and others. This is the point at which we transfer the merits of the Mass. In Buddhism it would come at the end of the liturgy, but the effect is the same. This "transference of merit" has been much misunderstood.

In the Middle Ages it was thought that doing certain good works, such as charitable giving, going to Mass, paying for Masses to be said, and so forth, gained one a number of merit points, like gold stars or smiley faces, which would offset all one's bad actions which had earned frowney faces. The game was to collect as many smiley faces as possible. Books were written which gave precise details of what would earn what, like a trading stamps brochure. With the right amount of effort one could come out even with God, and then an extra push would put one into the black, with what were called "works of supererogation," or doing more than one was asked. Any smiley faces one did not need could be given up and tagged with someone else's name, particularly the name of someone who was dead. Priests made a lot of this, for they got the funds for Requiem Masses. You wouldn't want to leave poor Grandma in Purgatory a minute longer than necessary, now would you?

The Pope decided that, coincidentally enough, one could get a bonus set of smiley faces by giving money to the Vatican. A Dominican priest named Fr. Tetzel went around Germany raising money for Rome in this way, repeating his formula, "As a coin in the coffer rings, a soul from Purgatory springs." This made Luther a very angry young man indeed, and came to be noted as one of the prime causes of the Reformation. Protestants therefore gave up all talk of merit except that of the all-sufficient merit which came directly from Christ as a free gift. Catholics have kept the idea around, but like a dreadful vase which was a Christmas gift from an aunt, it has been more and more pushed aside without actually being thrown away. But there is really nothing wrong with it, if we ask the Buddhists to explain it to us.

It turns out that both Protestants and Catholics have been treating merit as if it were a physical object. But Buddhists tell us it is, as is really quite obvious, a mental phenomenon. Physical objects obey physical laws, and are rightly bound by the law of quantity. If someone gives me an orange, and I give it to you, I no longer have an orange, and there never has been more than one orange involved in the process. Mental phenomena obey mental laws, and are unconstrained by the law of quantity and the law of the conservation of energy—in fact, they reverse these laws. A TV commercial for a brand of shampoo (or is it a hairspray?) says, "I told my friend, and she told her friend, and she told her friend, and so on, and so on, and so on . . . ." until the screen fills up with happy women whose hair is just right. Information, a mental phenomenon, increases by being passed on. I do not lose the ideas I am writing down by virtue of giving them to you in this book.

The same is true for sadness, joy, or love. Buddhists say that religious merit is like joy. By performing a certain good act or liturgy, a person generates joy, and this joy is made more by being passed along for the good of all beings, or for the good of one being in particular, such as Grandma, who has just died. Therefore, it seems eminently reasonable to me for a Catholic to dedicate the merit, the joy (which need not be a superficial happiness but a deep sense of rightness) generated by doing such-a-thing (as, for instance, attending Mass) to so-and-so for his or her well-being, in a formula such as "This Mass is being offered for my baby sister, who is ill." Looked at in this way, merit is an aspect of the loving intercourse between God and creatures (a point the Protestant Reformers emphasized) and, like love (a point which neither Protestants nor Catholics seem to have noticed), can be felt to increase or decrease but has no sense of precise calculation about it. Luther and Tetzel, wherever you are, please take note.

After the intercessions, the Mass naturally moves us into the next room of the mandala, very close to the Cenacle. In the Protestant tradition, it has become normal, out of a fear of doing something Catholic by mistake, to stop the motion of the Mass at this point and tautologically call their liturgy "A Service of Worship." In Sweden they even call it High Mass (*Högmässa*), and the priest (the Church of Sweden is Lutheran but has preserved the Apostolic Succession) wears a chasuble. I hope it is now clear that such a truncation renders the whole endeavor meaningless. It is like stopping a symphony at the end of the second movement or, to revive the candid imagery of the medieval mystics about which we are today so squeamish, like coitus interruptus. I appeal to my Protestant brethren (if any have made it this far after my dismissal of Barth) to bring back liturgical integrity to their services by restoring the Lord's Supper to its rightful pride of place. We are a long way from the Reformation, much further, I think, than any of us realize, and there is no reason to cry "Popery!" now at something which might have been popery then.

We, at least, will go on.

D. I AM FOOD: THE STATUS OF DEITY

In the early Church, everyone who had not been initiated (baptized) was dismissed after the Liturgy of the Word, and the doors were locked. The central part of the Mass, the Consecration and Communion, took place in secret. Unfortunately, reports about flesh and blood being consumed leaked out, and it was decided by the pagans that Christians ate babies in their private rituals—luscious, chubby, innocent pagan babies, and this made the pagans quite upset. (Pagan, by the way, used to be a noble word, and so I employ it here.)

The stress on secrecy is understandable. Many other religions at the time kept their important ceremonies secret. Mithraism, which was a serious competitor with Christianity, had a liturgy which looked superficially like the Mass, for it centered on the eating of bread and the drinking of wine, and it held it in a natural or artificial cave called a Mithraeum, entrance to which was barred to uninitiates. These caves have been found throughout the Roman Empire, even as far north as Hadrian's Wall in England. Some religions, such as Orphism, were so secret that their rituals have perished with them, and we can only guess at what might have gone on. Secret rituals are also found elsewhere, especially in Hindu and Buddhist Tantra, and in some forms of Taoism. Americans who become initiated into TM are told that they must not reveal "their" mantra.

This kind of thing seems to have outlived its usefulness. Secrecy heightens the sense of separation between the sacred and the secular, the initiates who know and the dumb robots who die like flies. If the Jungians are right, and humanity as a whole is growing up in an analogous way to that in which each individual human grows up (Erich Neumann, *The Origins and History of Consciousness*, 1954), then we may be moving away from this secretiveness. Children love to form little bands which have their own special secrets, communicating with each other in code without, they hope, adults and other children knowing what they are doing. A mature adult feels that she has nothing to hide, that she does not need to protect her ego from dissolution, and she adopts the openness of "Mi casa es su casa."

So it is that today anyone can go to all of the Mass, and indeed a Christmas Midnight Mass without at least one drunk at the back calling out unsuitable phrases, seems to have something missing. The secrets of the Tantra are now becoming available to more and more people who have not had the traditional preparation. Mandalas which are supposed to be viewed only under the most restricted circumstances have

been printed in glossy art books and may be glanced at during
cocktails and the TV news. Scholars are laboriously recon-
structing and publishing hidden or forbidden gnostic and
magical texts. Selections from the Zohar, a Jewish mystical
text that was forbidden to any but over-forty, married males
who were punctilious in the observance of the Torah, are
now available at paperback bookshops. A Buddhist initiation
which I received was formerly reserved for Tibetan monks of
at least twenty years' standing, but was offered in Wisconsin
by well-known and respected lamas to anyone who seemed
earnestly interested and had the necessary dollars, although
the traditional curses upon those who would reveal the details were not omitted.

What I think is happening is that, as we mature, the sharp
division between the sacred and the secular is breaking
down. It is *de rigueur* for the Popes, at rather frequent inter-
vals, to lament the secularization of the sacred. They do not
seem to notice the sanctification (or "sacralization," to use a
University of Chicago term) of the secular. The modern mystic is what Neumann has called a "world-transforming mystic." He does not seek to escape the world, as was common
in Gnosticism and its medieval descendants, he seeks to
make a heaven on earth. Often he is de-institutionalized. All
those marchers against nuclear power, strip-mining, and social injustice would have been unthinkable in the Middle
Ages. They are for a better planet, and whether it be Christian, Buddhist, or Native American is of no consequence to
them. Just be cool and feel the vibes, man.

Thomas Merton is an interesting symbol of our times. At
first he fled his bohemian youth for the strict solitude of a
Trappist monastery, but later he felt himself to be a "guilty by-
stander" and tried to move, though never very successfully,
toward a this-worldly mysticism.

There may indeed be a general movement toward an insti-
tutional condition of centers without identifiable boundaries.
Some people are talking of "churchless Christianity," even

"religionless Christiantiy." Others speak of "the sacralization of Science." Such a "ripple model," locating the spot where the stone enters the pond but not taking a firm line on where the ripples die out, is how Buddhism views itself, and it is not incompatible with Christianity; it is indeed very much the way Orthodoxy has conducted itself. The center is the Trinity actualized wherever the liturgy is celebrated.

Hence it is appropriate for us today, as we approach the most sacred part of the Mass, to feel the walls of the church building dissolving, and to invite into it, in our imagination, all humans of all races and creeds, all the animals and plants and seas and mountains, not into a shuttered Noah's Ark, but into a joyful center of transformation, burning with the creative love of the Trinity. This we begin to do at the Offertory.

1. THE OFFERTORY:
THE HUMANIZED UNIVERSE MANDALA

There is a story of some Christians stranded on a desert island. Sunday came round, and they wanted to have a religious service. "Can anyone say a prayer?" No one could remember one. "How about a hymn?" No one knew one. "Well, we must do *something* religious. Let's take up a collection."

If they took up the collection properly, the people in the story would have been very religious indeed. The actual gathering up of money (or goods, in cultures whose economy is not based on money) is necessary, but it is only a symptom of a much grander thing that is going on. If you can afford to give money into the collection, and (if it is a special collection) you have no objection to the cause, it is an insult to yourself (as you may see in a moment) not to give according to your means. But if you honestly cannot afford anthing, you can still participate in the *attitude* of the Offertory.

The Offertory reminds us that, in the world of the Spirit, as in the physical world, "there ain't no free lunch," although the laws of buying lunch differ. As with the interchange of merit, the interchange of offerings between God and creation does not depend on quantity but on quality. Spiritual offerings are, like life itself, antientropic (they produce more energy than they consume).

Buddhists say that the best gift is the gift of the Teaching (the Dharma), because with it one attains liberation. In comparison with this gift, others are paltry. Yet when one goes for an interview with a lama, one is supposed to take with one a paltry gift, like an orange, in exchange for the deathless Teaching that he will give. By giving the orange one is saying, "I'd like to repay you for your kindness in helping me with my problems; I'd like to give you the whole world, but I don't own very much, so how about an orange?" The orange is the vehicle of one's *attitude* that one is giving all one has. This seems to be the point of the story in the Gospels, where Jesus commends the widow (note that widows did not have social security then) for giving a tiny gift because, whether or not it was *really* all she had (the story may have been fixed up to make it more dramatic), Jesus recognized her sincerity as against the carelessness of the richer people who gave simply out of habit (Mark 12:41-44; Luke 21:1-4).

The primacy of attitude in spiritual giving, the principle that "it's the thought that counts," has an important consequence. One *can* give the whole world. Before a lama gives formal teaching to a group of disciples, the disciples offer him the world in the form of a Universe Mandala, which may be given either as a physical model or as a mental visualization. The traditional Buddhist cosmology has already been mentioned above. Here I want to go into it in more detail because I have found it a help in participating meaningfully in the Offertory.

A world-system is regarded by Buddhists as round and flat like a plate, resting on space. Its rim is a circle of tall iron mountains. At its center is the immense mountain called Meru or Sumeru, which is so high that, in comparison, all earthly mountains seem as flat as Kansas. This mountain is the home of the deities, and it has four faces each made of a different jewel. Around Meru are seven concentric rings of lesser, but still very high, golden mountains, and in between each range is an ocean which is always calm. Midway between the outermost range of gold mountains and the encircling ring of iron mountains there are four continents placed symmetrically at the four quarters. Each continent is a different shape and supports anthropoid life-forms whose heads are the shape of their respective continents. There are two minor continents flanking each major continent. All the continents rest in the Great Ocean, which is subject to storms. The sun and moon circle the world-system, passing over each continent in turn. Humans live on the southern continent, which has the shape of an inverted triangle (like India, where this cosmology was thought up), and our heads are shaped like our continent. When we look up, we see the southern face of Mount Meru, which is made of sapphire, and so we say that the sky is blue. A rough diagram of this, omitting details and the Sanskrit names, may help (Figure I).

It is this mandala which is offered to all the Buddhas of the past, present, and future in the person of the lama who is about to teach. I find that this practice helps the Offertory at Mass to become more than just the setting of a table which, of course, it also is. But the table of the Mass is not just *a* table, it is *the* Table, the Cosmic Table.

What can we offer God, if he is the source of all? Not even an orange. Buddhas do not create anything, so we can offer them things which are truly our own. A Christian cannot offer anything which he has made independently of God. And this is where Christ comes in.

A Christian's offering begins in a similar way to a Buddhist's offering. He gives everything there is, the Pearl of Great Price (Matthew 13:46), which is nothing less than the entire

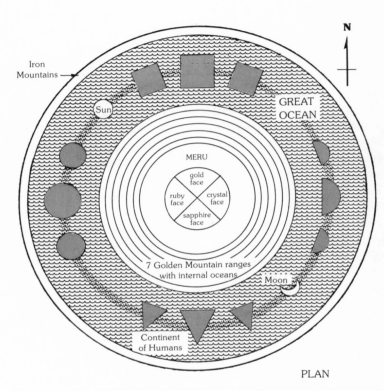

Fig. I. A UNIVERSE MANDALA

universe, back to the Creator who gave it to him. He then adds his own human dimension. Not only does he offer the wildness of the uninhabited mountain peaks and ocean depths, but he also offers his cultivated crops and their products—specifically, he offers bread and wine. The activities of agriculture, baking, and wine-making are a co-operation between, or co-creation of, God and humans. The Greek Orthodox call this *synergy*, or "working together." St. Teresa of Ávila said that God has no hands, feet, voice, and so forth except ours, and through these he works. This is why the priest says, at the Offertory, "Blessed are you, Lord, God of all creation"—this phrase comes from an ancient Jewish blessing which is still in use—"through your goodness we have this bread to offer, *which earth has given and human hands have made*." The blessing over the wine is similar.

The Christian, then, offers a *humanized* Universe Mandala. But that is not all. The priest adds that the bread and wine will become "the bread of life" and "our spiritual drink." The humanized universe is about to become, in Christ, a divinized universe. As a warning that this is going to happen, the priest mixes some water in with the wine. Originally, this was merely a sensible precaution to make it drinkable, since it seems that ancient wines were pretty rough. But it came to be regarded as a symbol of the sharing between Christ and humans of divinity and humanity. To keep things in proportion, only a few drops of water, symbolizing our humanity, are put into the greater bulk of the wine, representing divinity. So the priest says, "By the mystery of this water and wine may we come to share in the divinity of Christ, who humbles himself to share our humanity." In the Orthodox liturgy, the water is warm, so that it "enlivens" the wine.

This part of the Mass starts off as a simple meal of basics— bread and wine were the coffee and doughnuts of antiquity —and ends as a communion of cosmic significance. A balanced celebration of Mass should display both aspects. The Tridentine Mass, when celebrated at the Cathedral on high feasts, glittered with cosmic significance, but was hardly very cosy. In reaction to this, some Masses today are so much of the "y'all come" variety that they are, as I have lamented, indistinguishable from a coffee break that happens to have bread and wine. If a Mass is going to make any sense, it must keep its two faces, the divine and the human, the awesomeness of the altar and the friendliness of the dinner table.

The Offertory, then, gives us our second Visualization. Form a picture of the world as the vehicle for any money you may be giving. The Buddhist universe is a good picture because it "fits" onto the paten or plate on which the priest offers the bread, and into the round mouth of the chalice. But if you staunchly object that the Buddhist picture is "wrong" (it is only wrong physically, it is an excellent shape mythologically), then you can visualize the blue globe of this planet as it appears from outer space. Come in occasionally, to either picture, for a close-up and visualize a mountain, a desert, some animals. Especially, see wheat and grapes, and flash on the general process of baking and wine-making. Then mentally offer the humanized Universe Mandala on a visualized paten and chalice which you hold as the priest physically offers the bread and the wine.

This mental offering is *just as important* as the priest's physical offering. Until recently we used to act as if the Mass were rather like the Superbowl, with the priest doing all the important things and the people cheering him on. Vatican II has reminded us that this has never been the Church's official view. We are all priests, or rather, some of us are given the title "priest," while all of us are involved in the priestly activity of mediating God to the world and the world to God. The man at the altar is acting in our name. He is the focus of our priestly activity, but he cannot function without us. For this reason, it is now forbidden, except under very special circumstances, for a priest to say Mass if there is no congregation. The "private" Mass of pre-Vatican II, with the priest whispering to himself and occasionally turning round to bless a non-existent congregation, is an evident absurdity.

The Mass opened with a greeting between "priest" and "people" to make it clear from the very beginning that we are all equally involved in the action. Then, after the Offertory, the priest washes his hands. This is another of those ritual baths which are taken before entering a sacred space and are so common the world over. He then says, "Pray, brethren [and sisters, we might wish to add], that *our* sacrifice may be acceptable to God, the almighty Father." For the sake of good order and to save on equipment, we delegate the *physical* responsibility of performing the central act to the "president" (as he is now officially called, because he presides over the Mass) by replying, "May the Lord accept the sacrifice *at your hands* . . .," but we are not in the least called upon to give up our *mental* responsibility of preserving the attitude of offering. By letting the priest do everything, and not even giving money when we can afford it, we demean and insult ourselves.

A woman who converted to Tibetan Buddhism told me she did so because it gave her something active to do, like a priest. She no longer felt like a passive observer as she had during her years as an Episcopalian. I was astonished that an intelligent and mature woman such as she had never heard about the priestly activity of the entire Church. It turned out that though she had heard of it, it had never been emphasized, and she had never been told anything specific that she might do to fulfill her priestly function. She felt more like a waiter than a diner.

This is probably the fault of the hierarchy which, having got a piece of the rock, tried to fool us so that we shouldn't have any of it. Anyone who felt the priestly urge was pressed, unless they had made the mistake of being born as a female, to "enter the Church" (as if they were somehow outside it).

Apparently I myself was insufferably pious as a boy, for I was advised "Why don't you become a minister?" (our family was Protestant at the time). Since I have always regarded adults as devious (making up improbable stories about ravenous sailors coming down the street who would eat up my rice pudding if I did not eat it first), I felt I was being manipulated and, though I came close a few times, I managed to avoid the clerical state. Now I see that the whole attitude was wrong-headed, and I endorse the words of a spiritually perceptive London woman who had been landlady to a stream of candidates for the Anglican priesthood. "Sometimes," she said, "a boy feels he is called to the priesthood, but actually he is being called to deepen his own spiritual life." And, although I am not myself opposed to the ordination of women, those women who desire ordination might test themselves against this remark, making the appropriate gender changes.

As, now, the president (as I shall from now on try to remember to call him) says the Prayer over the Gifts, send your visualized Humanized Universe Mandala on to the altar. Then, as he repeats the greeting of priestly binding ("The Lord be with you"), allow the visualization to rise out of sight. Something else is going to happen.

2. THE ACCLAMATION: ASCENDING THE MOUNTAIN
The ascent of the Mountain now begins. The president asks us to lift up our hearts. What we do in fact is to raise our whole bodies, in our imagination, to the center of the Mountain-Palace-Mandala.

Although God is placeless (everywhere and nowhere), it is useful to regard him as sitting on top of a mountain. We naturally think of "better" as "up." The head of a company has his office on the top floor of Consolidated Conglomerates, Inc. A king's throne is set on a dais. The head is more honorable than the feet. People climb a mountain not simply "because it's there" (which really is not much of a reason —people do not step in dog droppings "because they're there"), but because it is high, and the higher the better. It makes them feel "on top of the world."

So we go up the Mountain of God, and what do we see? Nothing, if we are truthful. We sing "Holy, holy, holy . . . ," a text which we take from Isaiah 6:3, where it is sung by beings who have a special set of wings *to cover their faces.* They fly around like bats, not seeing the God whom it is their only function to worship. If God is the Source, how much energy must he have? When someone looks directly at our sun, he goes blind. Yet the sun is a minor star in a vastness of galaxies. How could anyone endure the concentrated energy of the creator of the whole universe?

Moses, according to one story, could see God only from the back (Exodus 33:23). We constantly come across the assertion that Pure Energy cannot be experienced directly. A Hindu myth tells how the gods decided to give the river Ganges to humans, so that they could grow crops. (The Ganges Basin is the only major segment of the Indian Subcontinent not dependent upon the unpredictable monsoon rains.) However, if they dropped the river straight from heaven, its force would destroy the earth. So, Lord Shiva volunteered to sit under it as it fell, and let it mitigate its force by spreading out in his hair. Thus it comes about that the place where the Ganges springs from the Himalayas onto the plain is called Rishikesh, "The Hair of the Holy One," and is believed to be a home of Shiva. Many spiritual teachers live there, and so it was there that the Beatles went for meditation instruction. Mystically, the Ganges symbolizes the pure Life-Force, and Shiva's hair is matter, in whose inner recesses we can see, if we look properly, the veiled light of Divinity.

The Muslim mystic Avicenna approaches the question from the other end, the human end. At the beginning of the spiritual life, our ordinary world suddenly comes alive, as if we had walked out of shade into sunlight. We begin to see things in the light of Allah. As we progress, we turn our eyes toward the source of light itself, and, staring into the burning Eye of God, we go intellectually blind. As the unknown author of the fourteenth-century English treatise, *The Cloud of Unknowing*, puts it, as we approach God we know less and less *what* he is and more and more *that* he is. The Rhenish Master, John of Ruysbroeck, says that we leave our intellect *and emotions* at the Door of the Presence. Zen Master Dōgen stresses the necessity of dropping off both body and mind if we would "understand" Emptiness. And St. Gregory of Nyssa notes that, when Moses was commanded to build the Tabernacle, the central, holiest place had no windows. "So," he concludes, "Moses saw God in the thick darkness." This was a purer seeing, according to Gregory, than Moses' previous visions of the Burning Bush and the Fire on Mount Sinai. It is a purer vision than the Pictorial Vision of the Trinity which I recommended as appropriate earlier in the Mass, during the Gloria.

This mode of "seeing" is technically called *apophatic mysticism*, from a Greek word meaning "to withdraw the shining." We first see God in the mode known as *cataphatic*, that is, "shining out," in images and all kinds of intellectual and emotional rushes. But everyone who has really "been there" reports that this is good, but preliminary. God is not like anything or anyone else. He just is what he is. The Upanishads "describe" the Supreme by negating everything that can be thought about—*neti, neti*, "not thus, not thus." God is, as another anonymous fourteenth-century English treatise, *The Epistle of Privy Counselling*, puts it, "not in sadness or gladness, in fasting or feasting, nor in any of the contraries whatsoever, but he is *hid between them*." The Buddhist Emptiness is neither "this" nor "that" nor a mixture, nor neither. It is Beyond, as color is beyond black and white, but not the negation of black and white. It is seen with a new organ which begins to function after everyday mind and emotions have been overpowered. Ideas and feelings about God, his "lights," are withdrawn. The result is a Nothingness according to ordinary consciousness and an Everythingness according to superconsciousness.

As the Preface is sung or said, allow yourself to rise up the Mountain and hear (even if it is a pick-up guitar Mass) the silent music of the angels.

Angels are sometimes a problem for us because we allow ourselves to get stuck on their pictures. As C. S. Lewis has said, modern angels seem as if they want to pat us on the head and say, "There, there, don't worry," whereas biblical angels were such a fright that the first thing they had to say was "Fear not!" Angels do not need wings. Wings came into the picture (literally) when the Jews returned from Exile, bringing with them the Babylonian idea that all heavenly beings were birdlike. But the Babylonians were on this matter a trifle simpleminded. Not everything that flies has wings. Hindu gods fly because they are lighter than humans, and Chinese sages ride about on clouds. St. Thomas Aquinas calls angels "pure intelligences" by which he means that they have minds but no bodies, and so are not limited by time and space. I can think myself into any place or time instantaneously, although my body remains here and now.

That angels should exist is more likely than that they should not. Biological life-forms, even on this one planet, are extremely diverse. A cockroach and a human have little in common besides their chemistry and their stubborn insistence upon inhabiting the same apartment. Why should mental life-forms be restricted to the human realm? Most religions say that they are not. Disembodied creatures, or creatures with bodies which are invisible to us, and whose effect on us is good, bad, or neutral, are reported by most civilizations. Muslims believe in a whole society of *jinn* (feminine *jinnī*, whence "genie") who exist in parallel to the visible human world and are mostly irrelevant to us, although they occasionally cause problems. The jinn and jinnī come under the same laws of God as do humans, and some of them have become Muslim. Angels minister to both societies. The Hindu, Buddhist, and Taoist universes teem with more invisible and partly visible beings than most science fiction writers would care to imagine. I find it entirely reasonable to believe that, as we ascend the Mountain, we pass through ranks of flaming, nonanthropoid beings, the fireworks of the atomic dance, until we come to rest before the Fire himself, the source of the Dance who, while being beyond motion and rest, somehow dances with himself. This is the Holy Trinity, who combines the dynamism of the Tao with the stasis of the Greek Unmoved Mover.

TO GOD IN TRINITY

Glory be to the Father and to the Son and to the Holy Spirit:
Moving in his gracious and appalling world-transforming dance
To the rhythm of uncreated harmonies:
The dance of the immortal source of every light
Who is void and darkness to our sight.

Immediately after the verse from Isaiah, the president sings, "Blessed is he who comes in the name of the Lord. Hosanna in the highest." This is the very earthly shout of the crowd which welcomed Jesus into Jerusalem as he rode as a king sitting on a donkey (therefore as a king of peace, a donkey being a particularly unmartial mount). The sentences remind us that the Christian God is simultaneously inaccessible, unapproachable Pure Energy, and a human who needed a donkey to get around. The deliberate crashing together of Isaiah's awesome vision and the seriocomic spectacle of God being cheered as he rode on a donkey forces us to realize the nature of the Holy Trinity as transcendent, immanent, transpersonal and personal, all at once.

The Mass now moves toward its most glorious and tragic

moment. We act out, or re-present, the timeless time in the Cenacle when Jesus gave himself to his friends, one of whom was a traitor, in a manner far more intimate than the closest sexual union. He became Food, and we become Food with and in him. The Eater, the Eaten, and the Eating interpenetrate.

3. THE EUCHARISTIC PRAYER: MYTH IN ACTION

The Eucharistic Prayer, or "Canon of the Mass," of which there are now four choices, concentrates within itself all the other prayers of the Mass. It is a microcosm, a little world. Each of the four options is arranged slightly differently, but each contains similar elements. There is praise of the Father, invocation of the Spirit, manifestation of the Son in bread and wine, intercession for the living and the dead, and mention of the whole Church on earth and in heaven for whom and by whom, as the total Mystical Body of Christ, the action takes place.

Eucharistic Prayer I is the oldest. It goes back, in some form, to at least the fourth century, and was, until recently, the only Eucharistic Prayer in the Latin Missal. It has for me the friendly quality of an old overcoat. Various saints are honored by name—Cornelius, Cyprian, Chrysogonus, Lucy, Anastasia —often I have no clear idea of what they did, but the recital has a pleasantly incantational quality. The intercessions for the living and the dead are split up and placed before and after the Consecration, like two wings of a mansion. It is on the whole a very satisfying prayer, and it is a pity that it so often yields to Eucharistic Prayer II, the "quicky." Like instant coffee, this is convenient on weekdays, but on Sundays, when we have more time, its freeze-dried efficiency is displeasing. Prayer III is a little longer, making a stab at a cosmic focus, but Prayer IV is undoubtedly the finest, a worthy partner to the venerable Prayer I. It places the Mass firmly in the context of Salvation History.

The main purpose of the Prayer is to re-present the actions

of Christ at the Last Supper. Taking bread and wine, and blessing God—he was a Jew, and Jews do not bless their food, they bless (give thanks to) God who provides the food —Christ said, "This is my body and blood—do this as my re-presentation." The Greek word used here is *anamnēsis*, and it is much stronger than the official English translation, "memory," would suggest. It does not mean remembrance or recollection of a past event, but bringing again (*ana*) into full consciousness (*mnēsis*). The events in the Cenacle occurred at a moment when historical time and mythic time intersected. They can be dated, but they also "never occurred" and are "always occuring" in the parallel universe of mythic reality which scholars call *illud tempus, "that* time." When we repeat the actions of Christ in St. Malachy's, there is also an intersection of universes. We live simultaneously in the world of a certain, unrepeatable and unique Sunday morning, and in the timeless time of the Cenacle. The president is Christ and we are the Apostles, and also, by the precise logic of superconsciousness which only seems odd to ordinary consciousness, we are Christ and the president is the Apostles. The Cenacle is "again-present," it is *re-presented*.

Thus, against a cosmic backdrop of the praise of God the Father, in the presence of all the glorified ones we call Saints, and remembering the whole Church on earth which celebrates along with us, we repeat the words "This is my body, this is my blood," and Christ manifests before us.

This manifestation is what Buddhists call Manifestation in a Vase, i.e., in a container of some sort. A Buddha can manifest as a human, if he sees that that would be helpful, but he can also manifest as a substance, if that would be more helpful. L. Austine Waddell, a feisty Surgeon-Major of His Majesty's Bengal Army, who wrote a now outdated book on Tibetan Buddhism, in which he made it seem very creepy, recorded a ceremony with bread and beer which he called "The EUCHARIST of BUDDHISM" in order to discredit it, and pictured it on his frontispiece. (He was the kind of muscular Protestant who considers that in order to show that a religious practice is superstitious, it is sufficient to demonstrate that it resembles something in Catholicism.) He was not, as a matter of fact, too far from the mark. In the ceremony, a Buddha or similar Entity is visualized as inhabiting a torma (a kind of Tibetan dinner roll) and a vessel of beer or wine. The torma and beer are then consumed, either physically or mentally, and the Entity is ingested to become nondual with the practitioner. From "manifestation in front" the practitioner has moved to "manifestation inside."

This is so similar to what happens at Mass that one either has to take poor Mr. Millman's view that the Mass is pagan stuff-and-nonsense, or Newman's view that the Mass picks up and Christs a religious mode which the Logos had suggested to Tibetan Buddhists. Naturally, I side with Newman.

At the words of Consecration, then, form an Emotive Vision of the personality of Christ entering the two "vases" of bread and wine. A Pictorial Vision at this point is not very appropriate, for you would have to visualize Christ standing on the altar and getting in the way of the president. All of the personality of Christ is in both the bread and the wine, because flesh and blood cannot be separated in a living individual, but you might try regarding the bread as typifying the sadness of Christ, the pain and the work he did and still does on behalf of all creation, and the wine as his joy.

In honor of the great moment when God becomes Food for us, some sort of reverence, physical or mental, is natural. This reverence conveniently fits with the response "Christ has died . . . ," which is a mini-Salvation History. St. Augustine, who apparently had a very live congregation, said that the response of the people was like a roll of thunder.

4. THE COMMUNION RITE: DIVINIZATION

We now prepare to enter the heart of the Mandala. The King of the Universe awaits us on his throne of Bread and Wine.

When a Buddhist first approaches a Mandala, she symbolically covers her eyes so as not to be blinded by its light. Only when properly purified, protected by an initiation and having received an invitation from the deity, can she remove the covering and enter. Similarly, a Christian does not rush immediately up to Communion, but makes a few final preparations.

First, we recite the Lord's Prayer. This is something all Christians learn in childhood, and they can gabble it off any time, on cue. It is worth much more thought than that, for it is the central prayer of the Christian praying, as the Church Fathers said, to Christ, in Christ, and as Christ. The Gospels record that Christ gave us the Lord's prayer as a model. Its earliest form seems to be in Matthew 6:9-15, and this is the version which we all know. Luke 11:2-4 smoothes out, as so often in his Gospel, the craggy Aramaisms into more standard Greek, while retaining the same basic meaning, whatever that is. It may come as a surprise to learn that, despite centuries of use, no one can be quite sure what it means. This is largely because Jesus spoke Aramaic but was recorded in Greek, and the two languages see the world differently. As an old Cistercian monk shrewdly told me, "The more languages you know, the more people you are." The English, Latin, Greek, and Aramaic versions of the Lord's Prayer are different people. I offer here a few suggestions on interpretation, and a recommendation as to how to use it is a mantra.

UNDERSTANDING THE "OUR FATHER"

1. "Father." Luke stops the address here, while Matthew goes on, "Our Father, the one in the sky." Luke has the main point. The Lord of All is our loving Father (not our Freudian, projected, castrating Father!). Matthew's picture language is all right if it is not taken too literally. As a child, I used to think of heaven as a big cloud. For some reason I saw it as pink, es-

pecially when visualizing its sacred rodents in the hymn "Gentle Jesus, meek and mild, / Pittie Mice in Plissitie." It was some years before I learned that the second line was actually "Pity my simplicity" and that Plissitie was not another name for the Pink Cloud.

2. "May your Name be sanctified." It was and is a Jewish tradition, as I have just mentioned, to "bless God." When God blesses us, he shows us his favor. This favor is sometimes regarded as a kind of "holiness stuff" which resides in sacred objects. In Islam, the rosary of the founder of a Sufi lineage is said to possess Allah's blessing or *baraka*. This idea of the "infection" of objects which have come close to a holy person leads to the veneration of relics in Christianity and Buddhism, and it is found in the New Testament (Matthew 9:20-21, 14:36; Acts 19:11-12). I heard once of a devout woman who held up a bowlful of rosaries in St. Peter's Square and, while the Pope gave a blessing, she stirred the rosaries with her hand so that the blessing would touch all the rosaries equally and not stick to just a few, like lumpy sauce. However, when we bless God, clearly we do not add to his glory. Or rather, we do not add to his intrinsic glory, but we add to its visibility by proclaiming it. "Blessed be God" is like saying "Blessed be the inventor of hot showers" on a cold winter's night. This is what Mary's song of joy means when it begins "My soul magnifies the Lord" (Luke 1:46). God doesn't get any bigger. She just wants to make more of him.

3. "May your reign begin." Matthew, and many respectable versions of Luke, add "as your will is carried out in the sky, so upon the earth." We pray that the sovereignty of God will bring order to our disorder. As Dante put it, "in his will is our peace."

4. "Give us today our *epiousion*-bread" (Matthew), or "Give us day by day our *epiousion*-bread" (Luke). This is the stickler.

What does *epiousion* mean? It went into Latin as *supersubstantialis* and was understood as "supernatural," i.e., the Bread of the Eucharist. But, begging the pardon of many mystics, this does not sound like the most probable original meaning. The standard English translation calls it "daily bread," understanding it as "don't let us starve," which is a very sensible, if not an entirely certain, interpretation. An ingenious solution proposes that it refers to the manna with which God fed Israel in the wilderness. The manna fell every day in portions sufficient for each day. But on Friday, a double portion fell, so that the Israelites would not have to break the Torah by working (picking up manna) on the Sabbath. So the line is made to mean "Give us today our bread for tomorrow," that is to say, "Show us that you are ushering in the eternal Sabbath of the end of time." Pick your choice.

5. "Remit our debts [Luke: "sins"] as we have remitted our debtors." This is easy. It's "there ain't no free lunch" again.

The Law of Karma (cf. Matthew 7:2; Mark 4:24; Luke 6:38; Galatians 6:7).

6. "Do not lead us into *peirasmon*," [Luke stops here; Matthew goes on] "but release us from *poneros*." This is difficult.

Peirasmon means a test. It may refer to everyday temptation, or it may mean the Big Test at the end of time, when even good Christians will have problems remaining faithful (Matthew 24:22, 24; Mark 13:20). *Poneros* means "evil," and that is the way we normally translate it. But it has a definite article and so it may mean "The Evil One," that is, the devil.

My solution to this jumble is to regard the Lord's Prayer as a mantra, part of which has a semantic, dictionary meaning, and part of which does not. We should not lightly abandon our critical faculties, but there are times when it is appropriate. Reciting the words which tradition tells us were the words of God himself, which come to us with the accumulated *baraka* of the centuries, we find that "the Spirit supports our weakness; we do not know how to pray properly, so he himself asks in nonsemantic noises [i.e., mantras]" (Romans 8:26, my translation). As we say this mantra, we act the part of Christ praying to his Father. We are one with our High Priest.

For some hundreds of years, there was the tradition that on certain occasions (such as the so-called Little Hours, the short monastic services which punctuate the working day) the Lord's Prayer would be said silently. The cantor would begin "Pater noster" ("Our Father"), everyone would bow deeply and think the continuation of the prayer to themselves, and then the cantor would end "per omnia saecula saeculorum" ("through all ages of ages"), as everyone straightened up. The Lord's Prayer was very clearly being used as a mantra. Today, this custom has been relevanced into audibility, although there is much to be said for it, seen against the planetary background.

Another way to bring out the mantric quality of the Lord's Prayer is by adopting the physical stance of Christ as High Priest. The president of the Mass says the prayer with his hands extended. This is a very ancient posture which goes back to the worship of the Sun God—one stood looking upward and spreading out one's hands to the all-seeing eye of the sun. It is prescribed for Muslims and it is recommended in the Talmud. It is not at all unlikely that Jesus prayed to the Father in this position, and it would be very appropriate for the whole congregation at Mass to express its priestliness by spreading out its hands as the Lord's Prayer is said. If the whole congregaton does not do this, you could still do it as an individual. If that embarrasses you, then you could visualize yourself as doing it.

The president concludes the prayer by an expansion, added by the Church, on the final phrase "Deliver us from evil . . . ," and we reply with a doxology found in some late manuscripts, "For the kingdom, the power, and the glory are yours" [the Orthodox Liturgy adds, "of the Father and the Son and the Holy Spirit"] "now and forever." "Forever" is a misleading translation of an apparent Hebrew or Aramaic original meaning something like "into the Timelessness," that is, from now, through time, up to the time when Time will end and Timelessness will "begin." Eternity is the reverse of a lot of time. It is the absence of sequential time.

Everyone in the church building is now One Praying Christ. In order to express this unity, we turn to each other and wish each other the Peace of Christ, with an appropriate gesture—a bow, a handshake, or an embrace. (Now is the proper time to reveal our names to each other, if we feel like it!) This Peace is not the superficial peace which is a mere absence of hassle. It is a profound sense of rootedness, the partly conscious feeling of fullness like the satisfaction one has a couple of hours after a good meal.

There is a popular Japanese doll for adults called Daruma. Daruma (Bodhidharma) took Ch'an (Zen) from India to China and, although he was an Indian, he is regarded as the first Chinese Patriarch of Zen. His doll or statue, which is used as a mascot, grimaces fiercely, and has huge round pop-eyes, for that is the way Caucasians appear to the beardless, narrow-eyed Japanese. The distinctive feature is his lack of legs. The story goes that he sat in meditation so long, his legs withered away and dropped off. Therefore he is egg-shaped. There is a weight in his stomach so that, no matter how many times he is pushed, he will return to his upright position. He is centered on his *hara*, the seat of consciousness which is said to be near the navel. Superficially, he moves, but at a profound level, he is unmoving. This is the kind of centeredness-in-busyness which we call the Peace of Christ. (See Figure II.)

Now, we turn toward Christ manifest in the "vase" and address him as the Lamb of God, as the president breaks the bread to symbolize the breaking of Christ's body in death,

Fig. II: *Daruma*

and drops a crumb into the wine to remind us that flesh and
blood are inseparable. The symbolism of the Lamb is biblical,
and as such it calls forth an Emotive rather than a Pictorial Vision. Biblical symbolism is frequently Emotive. For instance,
the Bride in the Song of Solomon is described as having eyes
like doves, hair like a flock of goats, teeth like pregnant ewes,
lips like a thread, cheeks like sliced pomegranates, a neck like
a fortress hung with armory, and breasts like a couple of deer
(Song of Solomon 4:1-5). The Groom on the other hand,
also has eyes like doves, but his cheeks are like a kitchen gar-
den of herbs and spices, his lips are lilies, his body and limbs
are of gold, ivory, jewels, and alabaster, and he looks like a
tree (Song of Solomon 5:11-15). It is impossible to make
any pictorial sense out of this. The author wants us to feel the
goodness, the "good vibes" of all these things, and combine
them into one happy emotion centered upon the Bride or the

Groom. So, when a cantata by J. S. Bach addresses Christ as "Lamb of God, my Bridegroom," it would clearly lead our meditations in a quite unsuitable direction to imagine that we had actually married a sheep. The Lamb is the symbol of Christ as he goes weaponless to his sacrificial death. By yielding to evil, Christ overcame it—"in order to be strong, become weak" as the *Tao Te Ching* says—and so the Book of Revelation calls the Lamb a Lion (Revelation 5:5-7).

Saying a last couple of prayers that we should be granted purification (we are never instrinsically worthy of receiving God), we look at the bread and wine as the president says "This is the Lamb of God." In the Orthodox liturgy he says "Holy things for the holy people." With that, we step toward the altar, the heart of the mandala, holding our Emotive Vision of Christ manifest in the bread and wine, receive Communion, and accept our own divinization as the Humanized Universe Mandala is returned to us as the divinized microcosm of Christ, and as such we are offered back to the Father.

We have eaten the Food, but the Food is God and has eaten us. St. Augustine writes that God said to him, "Feed on me, and I will not be like ordinary food, which you will change into your substance, but I will change you into my substance." (*Confessions* 7:10, my translation.) At this stage there is no *discernible* difference between God and ourselves. We sing the Song of Communion from the Upanishads:

> I am Food I am Food I am Food;
> I am the Eater I am the Eater I am the Eater;
> I am the Eating I am the Eating I am the Eating;
> I am Firstborn of the Worldforce;
> I am prior to the gods;
> I dwell at the Eye of the Deathless;
> He who gives me is me indeed;
> I am Food; the Foodeater I eat;
> I have won the world and her spawning;
> I am burning like the sun!

But there is a subtle, very important difference between the Christian and the author of the Upanishadic text. It is the difference between monism and monotheism. A monist says "All is One" and reports that he feels *no difference at all* between the Lifeforce *as it is* and his own "soul." A monotheist says "God is One" and reports that he has *been adopted* by God so that he *feels as if* there were no difference between his soul and God. The symbol of monism is the dewdrop merging into the ocean. The symbol of monotheism (as St. John of the Cross gives it) is the window pane perfectly suffused with sunlight: the sun (God) and the window (the soul) are different, but their light is one.

The Christian after Communion can truly claim to have become God, but cannot claim to be God *in his own right* but only *by the action of the One God.* Baptism, and thereafter Communion, is the implanting of a holy seed, a baby Christ, which Blessed Isaac of Stella prays "may grow strong and immense in us unto perfect gladness and joy." Like the Taoist with the "Immortal Embryo" (*Tao t'ai*) and the Buddhist with the "Buddha Egg" (*Tathāgatagarbha*), we contain perfection and we must perfect it. We are gods, but we are baby gods. Until our thoughts, words, and actions perfectly conform to the thoughts, words, and actions of the One God, we are not fully divinized in all our parts. That divinization, Christians say, does not occur until we reach heaven. And then we go beyond dualities.

MORNING

See the eyes sparkle
in the open face of God,
passionlessly rising
upon just and unjust.

             Clap your hands twice:
             who now is looking?

After you have returned to your seat, remain as silent as possible and allow your mind to calm down. Do not "blank" your mind: there is no advantage in trying to give yourself a frontal lobotomy. As the Sōtō Zen people say, do not try to think and do not try not to think. Just be in the moment. You are Christ radiating from your heart God's compassion to all creatures. As more and more people receive Communion, experience the church filling up with Christ's all-radiating compassion.

This experience is called by Tibetans "Pride of Deity." The term was chosen with care, and it must be understood with care. Pride, especially spiritual pride, is a major transgression in Buddhism which can land one in the lowest of the hells. Pride of Deity is a major virtue which leads to nirvana. The difference is that between a particlelike ego and a spacelike ego. Our ordinary ego is particlelike. Buddhists call it the *ātman*. We locate it in time and space, and we protect, nurture, and aggrandize it. Pride of *ātman* leads to suffering, because it is a silly attempt to protect something which is *not there*. The true ego is spacelike, called *anātman*, and it does not have a location in space and time, although for convenience we tag a certain consciousness-flow with the word "I." Pride of *anātman*, of Emptiness, of Deity, is liberating because it is infinite, with no borders to protect. It is infinitely vulnerable, yet infinitely fearless. Both Buddhists and Christians test the genuineness of Pride of Deity (which Christians say arises upon the "crucifixion" of the old self such that, as St. Paul says, "The 'I' who lives is no longer 'me' but Christ who lives in me" (Galatians 2:20, my translation), by its effects or fruits: it produces compassion and selflessness. The least hint of hate, indifference, or selfishness is a reversion to impure or sinful pride.

When we can experience our ego as spacelike, we can put all our energies into helping others, and preserve ourselves from self-pity, self-hate, and deep depression. Deep depression is a symptom of experiencing our ego as particlelike. It is a positive emotion in that it is a stage up from the Slumberland of the Robots in which most of us live, but it is negative in that it is an awakening to an illusion. This illusion shows itself by the fact that, while mild depression can be cured by chatting to a friend, deep depression is worsened by this. The more we are told that we are worthwhile, the more we *know* that our friend is lying to us, that we are truly worthless. The logic, it seems to me, goes like this:

1. Significance is directly proportional to physical size.
2. I am finite.
3. The universe is infinite.
4. Therefore, no matter how big I become, I will always be insignificant.

We find this argument compelling because the *process* of its logic is impeccable. The conclusion follows ineluctably if the premises are true. But that is the point. The premises, statements 1 and 2, are false.

Significance has nothing to do with size. Whales, humans, and bacilli are all necessary for the universe. A bacillus called *Pasturella pestis* wiped out one to two thirds of the human race in the Black Death. The motion of the galaxies mimics that of the atoms. The universe is evidently concerned with *structure* rather than with scale. As the punchline of that surprisingly philosophical movie *The Incredible Shrinking Man* goes, "I understood," the Shrinking Man says as he shrinks to molecular size and escapes from the spider into the night sky, "that God takes no account of size."

Further, "I" am not of any size at all. It hardly needs St. Augustine, who wrote a ponderous thing on the size of the soul, to tell us that mind and ego do not have a physical size. They are spacelike.

Therefore, the argument is what logicians call "valid but false." It fails by defect of the premises. The extent to which I feel *my own* egoic pride or pain is a test of my spiritual development, of how the baby Christ is evolving and growing in me. As he grows, I become more and more sensitive to others' pain (I can cry when I hear of deaths on the TV news) and less and less to my own (I do not become embarrassed if I pour ketchup in my coffee in mistake for sugar).

The union between the soul and God in Communion is so close that the great mystics have not hesitated to use sexual imagery and to call it the Spiritual Marriage. The Hindu myths of Lord Krishna and his ladyfriend Rādhā are X-rated, and Christian monks often wrote spiritual commentaries on the Song of Solomon, to which, it seems to me, it is appropriate to open the Gideon's Bible on vacating one's motel room. The *Spiritual Canticle* of St. John of the Cross is the best known of such commentaries. We might explain this today as sublimation. The energy of sex, which is the most powerful energy of adult humans, is turned away from other humans and directed toward God, and there is a structural correspondence between the two activities.

CHRIST'S MARRIAGE BED

Come down, my Lord,
onto this bread,
into this cup,
and fierily inhabit
my morsels offered:
by this slight meal
furiously burst the bounds
of what I see and measure.

Come up, my love,
onto this bed,
into these arms,
and fierily inhabit
my body offered:
by this slight deed
furiously burst the bounds
of what I see and measure.

Somewhere,
innergalactically,
is there not bright Light
lovelorn for our souls?

The end result, of course, is silence and rest.

E. LIVING THE MASS

There is very little of the Mass left. Having brought us so close to God that he has entered into us and we into him, its purpose is largely done. There is a brief prayer of thanksgiving, once again the greeting of priestly binding, a blessing, and the dismissal. The blessing reminds us that, although we have just been divinized, our divinization is not yet perfect, and we still need to grow in the favor of God. While receiving the blessing, we bow our heads in thanks.

The Dismissal takes one of three forms, all of which are more or less desperate attempts to translate the Latin "Ite, missa est," which is the nonsense sentence "Go, it is the Missa"—whatever a Missa is. It sounds as if it means something like "dismissal," so "Go, it is the dismissal," a sort of "That's all, folks!" It seems that people were so relieved to get out of church that they called the whole service the Missa, from which the English word Mass is derived. So we quickly reply "Thank God!" and make for the door as fast as possible so as to be out of the parking lot before the rush, or, if it is raining, to be able to select an umbrella of superior quality to the one we had on entering.

Another way of looking at Missa is to say that the whole point of it is to send us out. "Your mission, should you decide to accept, is to transform the universe." We can regard the Incarnation as the beginning of an infection, an infection that heals. Christians are those who are brought into the risen humanity of the divine Christ and they are to go out to touch the troubled world, taking to it Christ's Peace. Like Mary, we have conceived Christ in ourselves, and we are to present

him to the shepherds and kings of our everyday lives. Not in
a pushy way, of course. Mary did not go around knocking on
doors and announcing "See my baby? *He's* the Son of God,
that's what *he* is!" But she did not hide him when people
asked for him. Christian missionaries have often given themselves a bad press because they have employed the hard sell.
Buddhist missionaries (except for the militant Nichiren Shō-
shū) realize that it is no good talking to a deaf audience. They
must speak of the Dharma if asked, but they will not speak of
it unless they are asked. All the Sutras begin with a request
that the Buddha should preach the Dharma. This convention
is followed liturgically by requesting the Master to teach. So,
if you hear a Buddhist sermon, it's your own fault. You asked
for it.

When the new Missal was being prepared, someone suggested that the unintelligible dismissal should be translated
"Go, live the Mass." This excellent suggestion was ignored.
But it is the only one that makes sense. Thanksgiving after
Mass does not primarily consist in saying the official prayers
of thanksgiving, but in *persevering at the heart of the mandala*. Whenever it does not interfere with our necessary duties
(don't, for instance, try this while you are driving), we should
visualize ourselves as adopted Christs on the summit of the
mountain at the center of the Palace Mandala, radiating
Peace from our hearts. This mountain is everywhere. As
Nicholas of Cusa says, God is he whose center is everywhere
and whose circumference is nowhere.

The Mass never ends, for it never began. It is a *way of being*
which we act out for an hour in symbol and then live out in the
ordinary world. The offering and receiving of the Humanized
and Divinized Universe Mandala resonates like an endless
song between Lover and Beloved, a living bond of flame. The
resonance becomes louder, the note purer, and the flame
brighter, as our love matures. We begin to see God in all
things, in glorious sunsets and in messy chewing gum that
sticks to our shoes, and we move into seeing all things in God.

God is The Best, says St. Anselm of Canterbury. He does not mean the best that there is, as in "You've tried the rest, now buy the best," but the best that *can become.* I find this definition of God most satisfactory for two reasons. First, he did not arrive at it as the conclusion to a chain of logical thinking within ordinary consciousness. It occured to him after a whole night of meditation, so it is more likely to have come from headquarters than from a branch office. Secondly, it is not really a definition at all, it is an exercise, based on the Latin tag, which I have above my personal shrine as a constant reminder to grow, "Deus semper maior," that is, "God is always More." Try it out with me. Think of the best that could happen to you. Fill it up with everything which you imagine would make you happy. But God is better than that. Repeat the process with better things. But God is better than that. Repeat the process with even better things. But God is even better. And so on, infinitely. The exercise is supposed to "blow your mind," although Anselm did not have the phrase in his vocabulary.

Anselm's brilliant definition of God was largely ignored. He was eight centuries ahead of his time. Today, something called *process theology* is troubling the ecclesiastical waters and making Anselm seem very modern. Traditional theology used Greek philosophy to make rational sense of the Christian experience of God. "Greek" meant Plato and Aristotle, who were the philosophical giants of the time. They both taught, although in different ways that do not concern us here, that at the center of the universe there was an unchanging entity called The One. Everything had a cause except The One, which was a Causeless Cause, or The Cause of Itself. The One did not have any qualities, it just existed. The Self-Existent One. It could not change, since it was perfect, and if perfection changes, it can only change into imperfection. So, also, It must have predetermined everything, or at any rate It must know all the future so that if It could speak, It would say "I *told* you so!," just after you had totaled your car.

This frigid Abstraction, which emerges with logical rigor at the end of a syllogism (or at least we thought It did, but later we found flaws in the argument), which doesn't sound as if It would be any fun to meet, sternly offered Itself to the Church as the intellectually respectable form of God. Many of the Fathers did not like It, but It was the only One on the market, and they tried to patch It into Christianity as best they could.

Someone read Exodus 3:14 and decided that God had said to Moses "I AM WHO I AM" in capital letters (yes!—look it up in the Revised Standard Version!) and with more than a hint of smugness. Therefore, God must be It and It had told Moses, "I AM THAT WHOSE ESSENCE IS EXISTENCE," which was not, of course, what Moses wanted to hear, and if God had really said that, Moses would have given him a sharpish answer, as he did later when God decided to abandon the Israelites. "How can you do such a thing already?" replied Moses, "What will the neighbors think?" God saw the point, and relented (Numbers 14:11-20).

As a matter of fact, God had gone to considerable trouble to reveal himself in Hebrew, and there was a reason. You cannot say "I am who I am" in Hebrew, because "am" is present tense and Hebrew does not have any tenses. It has incomplete and complete *modes* of the verb.

English has a mixture of tense and mode, but it is not very clear about the difference. If someone comes into my office and asks, "Are you on your bike today?" I might reasonably reply, "No, I'm in my chair," at which point she will throw a piece of chalk at me. What she meant was, "Are you in the condition or mode of being a bike rider today?" (the verb "to be" in the incomplete mode) and I had replied "I am here in my chair" (the verb "to be" in the present tense). God said to Moses, in Hebrew, *eh'yeh asher eh'yeh*, with the verb in the incomplete mode. The best way to translate this into English is to use the continuous present (similar to "I am on my bike"), thus: "I will always be with you." This was what Moses wanted to hear because he was going to have a series of distressing run-ins with Pharaoh, and he wanted to be sure he had the trump card.

On these three Hebrew words (four in Latin, five in English) an enormous theoretical edifice was built called Christian Theology. But it was always an expensive building to maintain. The roof kept leaking, it was draughty, and terrible Things kept escaping from the basement. The roof leaked because the God of Christian experience, the God of the mystics (whether the mystics were famous monks or nuns, or unknown peasants), was always trying to break in on the fixed Cosmic Top which the philosophers had so painstakingly constructed. It was draughty because we could never keep all the windows closed at the same time. For instance, if God is all-knowing, all-good, and all-powerful, then he must know we are going to sin. In his goodness he would wish to stop us, and in his power he could stop us. So, we are robots programmed to do good. But in fact we see that we do not always do good; in fact we very often do very evil things indeed. So, we cannot be robots, and there must be free will. If there is free will, we can sin, and God cannot stop us, so he cannot be all-powerful. But when we do sin, he sends us to hell, so he cannot be all-loving. And yet, God is all-knowing, all-loving, and all-powerful. As soon as we shut one window in this Munster Family mansion, another flies open.

I believe it was the tiresome apparitions of the Things from the basement that finally caused many theologians to move out of the house. The dynamic God of revelation was not only leaking in through the roof, he was erupting out of the ground. He seemed to be *growing* or evolving. The Perfect It would never be so badly behaved as that.

In the Middle Ages, society was relatively stable, and short human memories were not assisted by accurate, extensive, and accessible historical records. Most people seemed content to believe that things had always been as they were then, and always would be. We identify a period called the Renaissance, beginning somehwere around the end of the fourteenth century, by the irretrievable breakup of this view. Change became more rapid, and so more noticeable. Merchants took over from aristocrats and challenged tradition by rising to prominence on their business acumen alone. Better texts, thought at the time to be the originals, of the Bible and the Greek philosophers, came to light, and printing made books generally available. It came to be worth the trouble and expense to learn to read, both for fun (knowledge) and profit (trade).

This trend has continued to the present, accelerating all the time. Since we are still trying to live in the Munster Mansion with its Unchanging Essences and Universal Laws, sudden changes make us nervous and we get "future shock." There is so much information, especially since printing gave way to electronic data banks, that it comes at us like a swarm of insects and we have to keep sweeping it away. A couple of hundred years ago, most people worked on the land. With the Industrial Revolution, there was a massive shift to factory work and city dwelling. Even so, the emphasis was still on production. Today, half the work force in the so-called "developed world" is in the information business. Book "writing" has become an affair of talking into a magnetic tape—an insult to the reader which I myself firmly resist. The resulting avalanche of loosely constructed semithoughts is, however, mercifully reduced by the Production Department to the blurb on the jacket, so that one is preserved from actually having to read the book in order to get the point. As a visitor once asked Dr. Samuel Johnson, "Have you read that book through, sir?" "No, sir," he replied in evident surprise, "do you read books *through*?" When every word had to be copied by hand onto parchment, and a Bible might cost the equivalent of an automobile today, an author had to say what he meant, and then stop.

In all this it is *change* which impresses us. Traditional theology cannot handle change. It makes the roof leak and its basement rumble. Many people with whom I talk have left

Christianity because of this doctrinal inflexibility. But, courage! Things are changing. Change is being taken seriously. By process thinkers.

Alfred North Whitehead, after a distinguished career as a teacher of traditional philosophy, sat down one day in his old age and began to write *Process and Reality*. It altered the course of Western thinking and, convergently enough, made Christian theology (although not in his hands, for he did not like religion) look very much like Buddhism. Whitehead imploded the whole Munster Mansion, reducing it to a brief cloud of dust, by the simple observation that Western philosophy had until then been a series of footnotes to Plato and Aristotle, and that there was nothing really compelling about the Platonic and Aristotelian systems. Before them, philosophy had been divided over whether reality was flux and nothing more, or whether there were fixed laws and unchanging essences beneath the flux. Plato and Aristotle had opted for the second view, which has a serious problem with anything other than superficial change, and got us all into a quite unnecessary lather scurrying about the Munster Mansion trying to keep it from changing.

Supposing we take flow seriously, as Ultimate. There is nothing behind the flow. Flow is. Flow flows. Change, then, would be expected. It would be necessary. We would seek to move the flow by means of the flow which is us, in useful directions and not in useless directions. We would seek The Best. We would not be in the least bothered by biological evolution, nor the fact that light appears to be a self-contradictory phenomenon, simultaneously particles and waves. We would be quite certain about Heisenberg's Uncertainty Principle. We would not have rigid laws like "Do not kill" which we then modify out of existence by finding circumstances (self-defense, war, etc.) where it means "Kill." Most importantly of all, we would have a *growing* God who, when blessed or "magnified," *would* in fact get bigger, in some strange sense of "bigger" (some non-spatio-temporal sense).

According to process theologians, who adopted and Christ-ed Whitehead's philosophy, God is infinite in his *potentiality*. He *can* do anything, just like the Munster Mansion God, but, unlike the Munster Mansion God, he is not capricious, telling you not to do something and then punishing you when he lets you do it. The *actuality* of God is finite and growing. The growing edge of God's self-actualization is an intimate co-operation ("I am always with you") between the free acts of creatures and the free act of God. A sort of cosmic bantering goes on between creatures and God, to find out the pathway for the developing energies that would be most fulfilling for both parties. This picture of God restores the warmth of the biblical God, who enjoys a good argument, and allows for both creaturely free will and divine control, without violating either. It does not solve everything, for indeed it is in the nature of flow to come up with new problems, but it gives us a theology that has Castaneda's "path with heart," and that is the only really important thing. *

Therefore, as you leave the Church Mandala after Mass, you move out into the next step that you and God will plan and take together. As you go about your work and among your family, friends, and enemies, you are working with God, living ethically and divinizing the earth, insofar as you direct the energies of situations along paths of fulfillment toward The Best, both for creatures and for God. As Father de Chardin has said, the only sin now is to block the evolving purposes of God.

*For an introduction to this way of thinking, see Robert B. Mellert, *What Is Process Theology?* (New York: Paulist Press, 1975).

THE SONG OF ALL SONGS

I remember,
long ago,
long, long ago,
the sun came up at midnight,
seen by no one but myself,
and my room was filled with light
and grew so huge
(Vimalakīrti, do you hear?)
that nothing was not there.

I sang from the Song of Songs
and the sun relaxed, and listened,
shining and still and blest,
and said, "Yes,
it is good, it is good, it is good."
The earth was made again,
the brown earth smiled,
and her creatures ran in her robes,
and there was great peace.

I could have called it Paradise;
yet it was but the forecourt —
an earnest of that endless day
(Abelard, is it true?)
in which the Saints embrace —
for the sun went down before dawn,
falling behind the dew and the birdsong,
and I walked on morning mists to Mass
like Lao-tzŭ riding the clouds:

long, long ago.

† may all beings be happy †

the pilgrimage of the mass: an outline for practical use

**I have designed this outline to help you remember the main points of my suggestions.

A. SETTING OUT
1. Read the texts.
2. Check on money for the Offertory.
3. Focusing verse: "I will go to the altar of God . . . ."
B. ENTERING THE MANDALA
Recognize the church building as a Location/Palace Mandala.
1. Porch: decompression chamber.
2. Holy Water: ritual bath.
3. Reverence to the center of the mandala.
4. Correct your motivation.
C. SPEECH
1. Introductory. *Status of Servant.* Abasement before the glory. Visualization of the Trinity. Dissolve/dismiss visualization.
2. The Word. *Status of Friend.*
   a. Readings. The story around the campfire. Prophecy; Proclamation; Wisdom Speaks.
   b. Homily. Look for and reflect upon one basic point.
   c. Creed. Hang out with it.
   d. Intercessions. Expand the joy to others.

D. FOOD
  1. Melt the walls of the church and invite the universe.
  2. Offertory. Visualize and offer a Humanized Universe Mandala. Dissolve/dismiss visualization.
3. Acclamation. Cataphatic Visualization of ascent; Apophatic Visualization of the Dark Fire.
  4. Eucharistic Prayer. Re-presentation of the Mythic action. Manifestation in front.
  5. Communion. Manifestation inside. *Status of Deity* with spacelike ego.
E. LIVING THE MASS
Persevere in the heart of the mandala.
Co-evolve with God toward The Best.

† may all beings be happy †